DARREN
CLARKE

An Open Book

MY AUTOBIOGRAPHY

with Martin Hardy

HODDER

First published in Great Britain in 2012 by Hodder & Stoughton
An Hachette UK company

First published in paperback in 2013

2

A CIP catalogue record for this title is available from the British Library

ISBN 978 1 444 75801 6

Typeset by Hewer Text UK Ltd, Edinburgh
Printed and bound CPI Group (UK) Ltd, Croydon, CR0 4YY

Hodder & Stoughton policy is to use papers that are natural, renewable
and recyclable products and made from wood grown in sustainable
forests. The logging and manufacturing processes are expected to
conform to the environmental regulations of the country of origin.

Hodder & Stoughton Ltd
338 Euston Road
London NW1 3BH

www.hodder.co.uk

To Mum, Dad and Chubby,
without whom I would not be where I am today

CONTENTS

ACKNOWLEDGEMENTS

The start of this book began 43 years ago and hopefully the final chapter of the life it portrays is still, hopefully, at least as many years into the future.

The first half of my story so far deals with the journey from Dungannon in County Tyrone, Northern Ireland, to Royal St.George's, Kent, and my finest hour. It has been a road full of joy and despair, cheers and tears, speed bumps and white-knuckle rides and would not have been negotiated without the help of many people.

There are too many to mention here and hopefully I have recognised their part in my life somewhere in the following pages. Please accept my humble apologies if I have left out anybody, but all know who they are and I am indebted to them.

Four I know who are mentioned deserve a special place here too because I owe everything I am and have achieved to them. My parents Godfrey and Hetty and sister Andrea sacrificed and supported so much when I was making my way through life and the golfing ranks while my manager Chubby has ridden pillion through all the journeys of success and failure, euphoria and sadness that form the backbone of my sporting story.

To all the sponsors who helped along the way please accept my deepest thanks and to my current benefactors, TaylorMade, Audemars Piguet, Dunlop Collection and Stuburt, I value your continued support immensely.

I also appreciate that there are people I know far less of who are responsible for this tome reaching the bookshelves. Not least is Hodder's Roddy Bloomfield, unparalleled in sport publishing with more than 1,000 books behind him and probably many more to come. Tim Waller also added to his own impressive collection of editing credits by dotting the i's and crossing the t's and ensuring my memory didn't play too many tricks on itself.

Finally, to my friend and colleague Martin Hardy for walking me through my life story and then assembling the bits and pieces into decent order aided by his research team Karen Davidson, Suzanne de la Perrelle and Harry Hardy, who was the first to recognise that my story has always been *An Open Book*.

PHOTOGRAPHIC ACKNOWLEDGEMENTS

The author and publisher would like to thank the following for permission to reproduce photographs:

Daniel Berehulak/Getty Images, Gary Cameron/Reuters/Action Images, David Cannon/Getty Images, Niall Carson/PA Images, Paul Childs/Action Images, David Davies/PA Images, Adrian Dennis/AFP/Getty Images, Stuart Franklin/Getty Images, Owen Humphreys/PA Images, Darren Kidd/Press Eye/Rex Features, Matthew Lewis/R & A/Getty Images, Andy Lyons/Getty Images, Tim Matthews/Action Images, Jaro Munoz/PA Images, Colm O'Reilly/Pacemaker Press, Bradley Ormesher/Mirrorpix, Pacemaker Press, Popperfoto/Getty Images, Jonathan Porter/Press Eye/Rex Features, Russell Pritchard/Press Eye/Rex Features, Reuters/Action Images, Jamie Squire/Getty Images, Ian Walton/R & A/Getty Images.

All other photographs are from private collections.

FOREWORD

by Lee Westwood

Where do you start with Clarkey? To me he is a cross between Ben Hogan and Hulk Hogan . . . and you never know which one is going to turn up on any given day.

The first time I ever saw him was at the British Amateur at his home course of Royal Portrush. He walked into the clubhouse with his blue-streaked, permed hair, wearing a brand-new pair of FootJoys and top-of-the-range weather gear. He displayed all the signs of being a superstar.

As a golfer, he's as natural as it gets. He has every shot in the book and one or two others, particularly when it comes to links golf. The closer to the sea, the better he plays. But even on parkland he is a formidable force, as his successes at the Forest of Arden and Akron demonstrate, and there are a fair few courses between those places and the nearest stretch of water.

There is no greater pressure in golf than at the Ryder Cup and yet when the stress is at its most intense I have seen Clarkey hit some of the best shots you will ever see. He can shape the ball both ways and when his tail is up and his confidence is high, he can hit anything and at whatever height the day and conditions demand. It is then that he has total control. But if you think I am painting a picture of a superhuman golfer, let me also assure you that when he's off, he's just like the rest of us.

Yes, he is human, but definitely not when it comes to shopping. He has no peer in that department store. Show him a mall and two hours later you will see a man carrying ten bags in each hand. On one occasion he bought sixty pairs of underpants in one hit. I know you will find that hard to believe, but it's true. I was with him when the attendant's jaw hit the countertop. And when he got back to the hotel he sat there staring at them, wondering how on earth he was going to fit them into his luggage. His play, be it good or bad, has never affected his ability to shop. And he's definitely an obsessive-compulsive – wanting the latest gizmos even before they've hit the production line.

I have been there through all the styles and colours of hair and clothes, but my all-time favourite was the outfit he wore one year at the Masters. I'm not really sure how to describe it, but the nearest I can get is to say that he looked as if he had been covered in glue and a gang of kids had thrown enormous M&M's at him. The pièce de résistance was surely the shoulder epaulettes.

My Ryder Cup memories of playing with Clarkey are many and varied, but none as vivid as what happened at the K Club in 2006 just a few weeks after his wife Heather died. The atmosphere all week was unbelievable. I think captain Ian Woosnam put us out last on the first morning because he knew the kind of reception Clarkey would receive and wanted all his other pairings on the course. Nobody could have known or guessed quite what it would be like, but it was the most emotional I have been on a first tee in my life. How on earth he made contact with the ball I have no idea, but he not only flushed it down the middle, but went on to make a birdie that not even our opponents, Phil Mickelson and Chris DiMarco, begrudged him.

If that one was made in heaven, then there was another the following day when we played Tiger Woods and Jim Furyk. We were three up with three to play; they were both in a good position to make birdie, I was in the water and Clarkey had a 25-foot chip. I was about 10 yards away from him as he chipped and when it left the club face I just knew it was going in. When it dropped for a certain half and the match, there was no doubt that Heather was looking down on him.

I've played with some of golf's biggest names in the Ryder Cup – Faldo, Montgomerie, García, Donald and Kaymer included – but Clarkey has always been my favourite to have alongside. You know that you can always rely on him. We get on very well, know each other's game backwards and never have to say sorry. And we've beaten the current one and two in the world on more than one occasion.

The only certainty about Clarkey is that you can never be quite sure what's coming next. He can have a 10-year-old head on and stomp around without talking to anybody and I have to snap him out of it by saying that if he was one of my children I'd tan his backside. On the other hand, if you were in the trenches you'd definitely want him at your side. You certainly would not want him against you, because once you get into Clarkey's black book, that's it. I call it Alcatraz – very hard to get out of.

Not only is he one of the most generous guys in the world, but he is also without doubt the best person to buy a car from. You know that he will never rip you off, and you can also bet on it that the cars will have every conceivable gadget. He absolutely loads them with extras and never does very many miles in them.

I'm sure he'll be telling you about the day he bought a trike and then ploughed it straight into the side of his house as soon as it came off the delivery van. That's him all over, along with the green, crocodile-skin Gucci shoes.

But what he won't be telling you, because until he reads this he won't know himself, is that when we opened a restaurant in Coleraine called the Salmon Leap, I once did a shift behind the bar and never charged anybody for the drinks. I could work the pumps but not the till. But I do know that the official beer of the jet we shared for a few years was Asahi Super Dry and we sank a few of those on our travels.

Nothing should ever surprise you about Darren Clarke. Watching him win the 2011 Open just about summed him up – it was so unpredictable and yet you knew it was always within him.

PROLOGUE

It was 5 a.m. on the Monday morning and the sun was starting to awake when we finally retired . . . not to bed, but to the kitchen. By now I could accurately claim to be tipsy – but I have never sobered up so quickly in all my life. I went into a blind panic. I couldn't see the trophy.

Where's the claret jug? What on earth have I done with it? For heaven's sake, where is it? Oh hell, I've lost it. I'm supposed to have it for a year, not just a few hours.

A quick scan of the house bore no fruit and definitely none of the claret grape variety.

After what felt like an age I remembered that at some point we had been at the bottom of the garden. There it was.

'Who on earth put it there?' I asked.

'You did,' Alison said.

Oh, you have no idea of the relief when we found it. It was probably trying to enjoy a bit of peace and quiet after being passed through a thousand hands and as many photographs.

By 6.15 a.m., Alison and I were the sole survivors and I was facing a dilemma. My morning-after press conference was due to start at nine and I wasn't sure what to do. If I went to bed, I might not wake up and even if I did I'd feel awful.

Then I came up with a cunning ploy. I knew the kitchen would be well stocked and, sure enough, there was the Red Bull just when I needed an injection of energy. And what better to accompany it than Absolut. It was 6.30 a.m. and I was drinking vodka Red Bull and still wearing the clothes I'd worn when I walked off the 18th green some twelve marvellous hours earlier.

At 7 a.m. it was decision time. Should I shower and change for the press, or go as I was? Chubby was up by now and I was afraid he was going to have a heart attack when I told him I was thinking of going in my work clothes. He made it perfectly clear that that would not be the done thing.

It was an easy decision in the end. I wouldn't look or talk any better if I did go to bed and I'd probably feel a whole lot worse, so I just jumped into the shower. I came out feeling refreshed – and even better once I was suitably dressed.

My eyes may have been a bit of a giveaway, but I didn't feel too bad as I set off across the field behind the house for the press conference.

On the way, I checked my phone and there were plenty of messages. Many major championship winners had sent 'Welcome to the club'. It was at that point that I fully appreciated that there's winning tournaments, there's winning big tournaments . . . and then there's winning majors. That's a bit different.

1

EARLY DAYS

It wasn't until I started researching my family tree that I discovered where my thirst came from. My mum Hetty's mother Hetty – at least they couldn't forget one another's names – was born into a family of Newry publicans, so perhaps they are to blame for my occasional excesses. I would also like to emphasise the word 'occasional', because although I have a liking for the black stuff and fine red wine, tales of my drinking habits far exceed reality.

My mum's father, Joseph McWhirter, was chief electrician in Dungannon's leading linen factory, but I can't accuse him of handing down anything through the genes from that particular area, because I know far more about when balls plug than three-pin plugs. Grandad Joseph and Grandma Hetty instilled a sense of family into all their offspring, and they were kept quite busy in that department because I have no end of aunts and uncles on their side. My mum was one of ten divided equally between boys and girls: Hetty, Desmond, Bobby, Samuel (deceased), Harry, David, Margaret (deceased), Mary (deceased), Joan and Linda.

On my father's side, there was Grandad Benjamin, while Grandma Ruby and her sister, Aunt Helen, had a bakery in

Coalisland, about five miles from where we lived in Dungannon, and they ran that for twenty years before retiring. My father was born in 1946 and christened Godfrey Benjamin, the middle name after his own father, and that name continues with my elder son Tyrone. The elder Benjamin died in 1982, and his wife Ruby survived him until 2010.

It might be difficult to imagine now – I would describe him as strapping and big-boned – but in his first year at senior school, Dad was not allowed to play rugby because, at a slim 4 ft 10 in, he was considered a bit of a waif. It was a look which did not continue, because he was soon an under-age member of the Under-13s. Although there was no football at school, he mixed that sport with rugby on leaving and played a couple of years for Glenavon in the Irish League. He started off as a reasonably mobile striker but ended up in defence.

After moving on to Dungannon Swifts, he also served a year as manager, but was far from enthusiastic about training, not a particularly encouraging trait for somebody in such a position. However, the team, who were in the Second Division at the time, did win the Intermediate Cup, which was then a big deal. Nevertheless, although still only in his late twenties, he decided he couldn't go any further in management and opted out of the sport completely. These days his interest in football is confined to supporting the team that plays on the other side of the park to my beloved Liverpool, but whose name escapes me.

My parents first met in 1966 when they were both in their teens. Mum was out walking her Alsatian, Rebel, and Dad really didn't take much notice of her at the time because he was more concerned about the snarling white teeth that were showing far too close an interest in his legs. A few days later, they met again at the local dance hall at a time when the country was going through a showband era. It must have been love at first sight, because they were married in the Presbyterian church a year later.

My father's first job was working for two of his uncles, who ran a fruit and vegetable canning business. He collected from local farmers, took the produce back to the factory for canning and then delivered to supermarkets and shops.

Sporting influences were not restricted to my father's side, however, because Mum's sister Mary was an international horse rider. One day she was out riding when a car approached from behind, tooting its horn. The horse reared, she was thrown off, hit her head on a stone bridge and was tragically killed. She was just 24 when she died on 24 July 1968. I was born exactly three weeks later.

Both sides of the family had come from a council-house background and that was where I spent much of my early life. We had a three-bedroom home with a kitchen and living room, before moving to another, bigger council house just 300 yards away, which also had a dining room and a bigger garden. The rent was £27 a week. My parents eventually bought the house and were awarded a percentage reduction, having been tenants for so long.

Dad, who had just one sister, Cynthia, moved out of the family business to work in the office of a ready-mixed concrete company.

In 1980, when the company relocated to Balbriggan, near Dublin, he went down south, returning home only at weekends. But in 1981 Dad's affection for golf attracted him to the greenkeeping side of the game and over the next three years he took all the examinations needed to help look after Dungannon Golf Club, loving the work despite the early-morning starts.

On my dad's side, the sporting connections go back at least another generation. His father Ben was a fearless and hard-tackling right-back whose potential was quickly spotted by Portadown. The Irish League side nurtured his talents until they found it impossible to turn down a bid of £2,500 from the English First Division club Sheffield United. It was a huge fee before World War II. Unfortunately, he was injured just before the 1934 FA Cup final, otherwise I might have had more sporting memorabilia from that particular quarter, although I am the proud owner of his Irish amateur international cap. His career, which included stints at Exeter and Carlisle, was eventually cut short by the outbreak of war. Grandfather Ben returned to play in the Irish League and then took a job in one of Dungannon's textile companies. It was fitting that he chose to settle there, because it is a town with a rich sporting history.

Surprisingly, the oldest club in the town is not connected to rugby or any sport commonly associated with Northern Ireland. Dungannon Cricket Club dates back to the middle of the nineteenth century, whereas the town's rugby club, although the sixth oldest in Ireland and a founder member of the Irish RFU, did not come into existence until 1873. And while Dungannon Swifts have excelled in the soccer arena, it is at Gaelic games that the town, which has also played host to hare coursing and greyhound racing in its time, has principally shone. I have been more than happy to add to the sporting tradition of an always proud if troubled area.

It wouldn't be a town in Ireland if there wasn't some interesting tale that locals love to tell about it. Dungannon's revolves around the unique former police barracks in the market square. It is said that the slightly eccentric design is due to 'a confusion' over the plans in Dublin. Apparently – although how much truth there is in the story I can only guess – the town ended up with a building intended for Afghanistan's Khyber Pass, while that current war zone got a barracks complete with a traditional Irish fireplace meant for the centre of our island.

And talking of the town's past, it was in April 1968, a few months before I was born, that Northern Ireland's first civil rights march took place, from Coalisland to Dungannon – the town later becoming one corner of the 'murder triangle' during the Troubles.

According to my mother, I was 8 lb 7 oz at birth and a very good baby. I had a shock of curly blond hair and big brown eyes and I'm told that neighbours and even strangers would stop the pram just to gaze upon this wonder of nature.

Apparently I wasn't like other kids. Whereas most children had something like a blanket as a comforter, mine was what I referred to as a 'dodi'; don't ask me why. It was the teat off one of my milk bottles, and I did tricks with it, putting it on the end of a finger or even my tongue and waggling it around. It stayed with me long after proper food replaced my milk-only diet.

Although I was a relatively good sleeper, something which remains with me to this day, there was one night when I wouldn't settle and I was brought downstairs and given a packet of crisps to keep me quiet while Mum and Dad watched a late-night movie. They certainly achieved that. In fact, they almost did far more. They very nearly killed me. I choked on a crisp and my mother panicked when I started to turn blue. We didn't have a phone and she ran out of the house screaming, 'What can I do?' One of her sisters lived just down the road and she headed there, but before they got back Dad had turned me upside down, smacked my back and eventually dislodged the offending crisp. Obviously, I have no recollection, but I'm told it was a terrifying experience for my parents.

It was not my only adventure as a youngster. I was something of an explorer and one day, at just fifteen months, shoeless and dressed only in nappy and vest, I decided to find out more about the neighbourhood. I crawled and then toddled out of the house, not stopping until I'd crossed the road and gone 150 yards down the street to Aunt Joan's house. I was totally unscathed by the experience, although Mum almost had a heart attack when she found out what I'd done. But she was smiling with pride the day I won a bonny-baby competition and then, as a three-year-old, when I again took first prize in a fancy-dress competition, wearing my grandfather's football kit.

My mum tells me that I was always a big baby, needing clothes that were two sizes up for my age. I never liked cheap clothes either and could tell the difference, because better cut clothes always seemed to fit me better. My love of driving things was also evident at an early age. A plastic American army jeep with a big star on the front was a particular favourite, along with the almost mandatory tractor and trailer.

By this time I had a sister, Andrea, and we are close not just by age – there are only eleven months between us – but also by nature. We got on well instantly, never fought, shared everything and were each other's best friend. She would later become my partner in crime, acting as lookout in my early teens, so that I could sneak a quick, prohibited smoke while she checked the garden gate for Mum and Dad coming home.

Ours was a house full of love but very little money. There was rarely any change left over at the end of the working week, but if there was, it was spent on clothes and toys for Andrea and me, particularly me. But Mum and Dad always saved enough to ensure we had a big present for Christmas to go along with a black bin bag full of bits and pieces. They sacrificed a great deal so that I could chase my dreams, and now that I am in a position to look after them, that's what I do and that's the way it should be.

Andrea and I also had two close friends, apart from Gary and Mandy, Auntie Joan and Uncle Roy's children, who lived just down the road. Our live-in allies were Sooty and Sweep, the glove puppets made famous by Harry Corbett. Sooty was a loveable but mischievous yellow teddy bear, while Sweep was an intellectually challenged grey Spaniel with long black ears. We carried them everywhere with us.

I owe Andrea a great deal. It must have been difficult for her growing up, because everything in the family appeared to revolve around me. I got everything and she got what was left, and that probably wasn't a lot. All the pictures in the house were me, me and me and it was always a case of Darren's doing this and Darren's doing that. I think she had it pretty tough, but it obviously did her no harm. I couldn't wish for a better sister and we are as close now as we were then. She lives nearby and looks after the boys when I am away.

I didn't have many friends outside the family circle, but Gary and Mandy, our cousins, often came with us when we went to our 'holiday home' – a £100 caravan with a stove in the middle. It was a getaway based in the middle of nowhere, close to Donegal. There were no recreation facilities for children, just the beach, although there was a golf course at Dunfanaghy, not far from where future Ryder Cup player Paul McGinley's people lived. I had no interest in golf then and didn't know Paul at the time. But I do remember the course, because all the greens were wired off to stop sheep and cows grazing.

We would often set off on the two-hour drive to the Marble Hill caravan site on a Friday evening, spend the weekend playing ball games on the beach, then return to Dungannon on Sunday night. It was fun for a while, but by the time I was 12, the romance of this almost ritual journey was over and boredom kicked in. I started to wonder what on earth the fascination with the place was. The message must have got through to Mum and Dad, because the caravan was sold shortly afterwards.

I was four when I started at Howard Memorial Primary School in Moygashel, two miles away, where Mr Graham was headmaster. The experience was not altogether a pleasant one. I was the victim of some bullying and got a few good hidings here and there, which forced me to keep myself to myself for quite some time. I told nobody, but Andrea knew what was happening, since it was usually on the way back from school towards my mum's parents' house.

Although I never complained, Andrea told Mum how I was getting a hard time at school from some older boys. Mum discovered who it was and one day when she came to pick me up in the family Volkswagen Beetle she spotted one of my assailants walking home. Mum stopped the car, jumped out, got hold of the bully, picked him up and popped him against the wall. I am not sure what her exact words were, but they were along the lines of 'You won't be doing that again, will you?' She told the boy that if he ever bullied me, then he had better watch out. From then on, I was never bothered by them or anybody else for that matter. Word quickly spreads in Dungannon.

My mother tells me she never had to discipline me, although I do remember getting on the wrong side of my father one Christmas after I'd been bought my first leather jacket. I wasn't totally in love with the style, so I decided to give it a little extra something. I went upstairs, took the chain off the plug from the basin and pinned it to the jacket. It was my acknowledgement of the punk era. Dad was so enthusiastic about this fashion trend that he gave me a choice – either I took the chain off and returned it to the plug, or the jacket would be returned to the shop. My flirtation with punk lasted all of ten minutes.

I'm told that Andrea and I differed in one way. Whereas I had a near-photographic memory, she had to study hard. I was considered naturally bright and could pass exams with the minimum of revision, while Andrea went to her room for hours, surrounded by reference books. I have a good and long memory to this day, as several people who have crossed me over the years know only too well.

My next educational port of call was the Royal School – a non-fee-paying day school in Dungannon. It is one of the oldest seats of learning in Ireland, among seven chartered by James I in 1608 to provide an English-style education to the sons of landed settlers, who were mostly from England and Scotland. Mr Forsythe was the headmaster and I received excellent reports, not because I was a swot or an egghead, but because of my ability to take in information and then regurgitate it on to paper when required.

Although my reports were usually pretty good, there was one aspect of me that caused a few problems with the teachers. From a fairly young age I was very much into experimenting with different hair colours, which did not go down particularly well with Mr Forsythe. I beat a regular path to the headmaster's office whenever I sported a different hue, and my backside also changed colour thanks to the administration of corporal punishment.

Normally if I knew I was in for it, I would take preventative action, or at least make sure it didn't sting as much, by pushing some extra layers of clothing or paper down the back of my trousers. The form of discipline employed by Ronnie Irvine, the chemistry teacher, was not so easy to nullify. I used to do all right in his class but messed about a bit, and his chosen punishment was to use a metal ruler on the hand. He'd turn it on its side so that the narrow edge was leading, purposely miss your outstretched fingers on the way down and then quickly come back up to rap you on the knuckles. I had to endure that quite a bit, but I don't think he ever hit me too hard, even though he had to be seen to be punishing me as much as everyone else in the class. The reason was that by this time I had already taken up golf, and Mr Irvine looked after all the golfers in the school and appreciated just how important their hands were.

Of the other teachers, I remember Mr Kirk – not so much for teaching us Latin as for possessing the bushiest set of eyebrows I had ever seen. He was a nice old man, but I doubt that I was his favourite pupil as I didn't like his subject. I was simply shocking. I never used to do any homework and always had to call somebody up when it was due, to copy from them.

If I didn't get Latin, I was equally dismissive of music and it landed me in trouble one week. Mrs Tully, I think it was, tried to get pupils to sing in the choir, but that kind of music has never been my thing, even though today I have a very eclectic mix on my iTunes collection. She'd get people up two at a time and try to figure out who could sing and who couldn't. I was to do a duet with classmate Eric Williams, but I don't have a note in my head and apparently neither did Eric, because when she instructed us to sing we didn't say a word and just kept our mouths shut. Her response was to put us in detention, but she never asked us again.

In general, I enjoyed school and although I'm sure Mum and Dad wouldn't have let me skive off anyway, I was never tempted to try. I did my best to balance schoolwork with golf and didn't take too many days away to play in tournaments, and when I did I always got permission. All in all, my school days were good ones.

I got eight O levels and two A levels. On the O list I got an A in English Language and an E in English Literature. Consequently, my command of English was pretty good, but I wasn't a great one for reading. I went into the sixth form to do geography, physics and chemistry – missing out on the pass mark for physics.

If I hated some subjects, I adored other things. My love of rugby union comes from my time at the Royal School, which had a rich tradition in that particular sporting discipline. The legendary lock forward Paddy Johns was a year ahead of me, so you can see the calibre of those attending. I shared Paddy's passion, if not his ability, for the game and played it all the way through school, captaining all the sides through the age groups. I was a No 8 or open-side flanker and also kicked – but despite being right-handed, hoofed the ball with my left foot, which was quite unusual. After captaining the Under-14s I was promoted to the second XV – a 15-year-old among boys mainly two years older. I was a tad slow getting off the mark, but once I was in my stride I took quite a bit of stopping.

I loved the game and couldn't get enough of it. My teacher, Mr Keith Patton, whose brother Fergie is still my solicitor back home, was not in the least bit pleased when I opted to drop the sport in the sixth form. Thankfully, there was an older head of sport there, Mr Ken Armstrong, who appreciated that however much I loved rugby, I was far more likely to be a success at chasing a much smaller ball around a field. He had played for Ulster, I think, and the game was also his passion. He'd cover for me if I ever had to play in tournaments. He could see that I had potential and wanted to help in any way he could, and if that meant watching my back when I had to opt out of school, then he did.

Although I felt I was always going to be a golfer, I did appreciate that a few subjects in the bank might be useful insurance. I wouldn't claim to be that intelligent, but I wasn't bad either. I never got into much trouble, but I once finished in a bit of a mess outside the gates.

I loved bikes and it was on them, after growing out of my jeep and tractor, that I discovered my need for speed. Unfortunately one day I was aboard my Raleigh Chopper coming down a steep hill when I realised I was going too fast, braked too fiercely and flew straight over the handlebars. I was kept in hospital overnight and released with no more than several bumps, scrapes and a bruised ego.

I took part in everything connected to sport at school and was actually allotted the very same house that my father had been in – Mountjoy. I must have had a strong arm even then, because I won the javelin competition, just like my father had done in his time there, but by this stage golf had gained my attention and I was never going to follow Steve Backley.

The likes of Greg Norman and Seve Ballesteros were more on my radar.

2

THE TROUBLES

Growing up in the heart of Northern Ireland in the era of the Troubles was something you just had to deal with. Bombs going off all over the place, people shot and killed, suspects tarred and feathered – it was all part of everyday life. Dungannon was a frequent target, possibly because the border with the Republic wasn't all that far away. I saw my share of everything that was happening, although in my early years I was never quite sure why the incidents occurred on such a regular basis.

The drums from the jungle telegraph came through loud and clear whenever there was a bombing or shooting. One of the most graphic scenes came after news filtered through that there had been shots fired and a car chase in the centre of town. A car had crashed just along Cunninghams Lane, close to where we lived. Being young kids, we all rushed across to see what had happened and arrived before the emergency services.

There in the back of the wrecked car was a man with a bullet hole in the top of his head, blood splattered around the interior of the car, the outside dimpled by gunshot. We weren't stunned or shocked, though. It was just one incident among many happening almost every day during those sad times.

All we were aware of as kids was that it was some sort of Catholic-Protestant thing, seeing as we were segregated at school and outside. One side of town was Catholic, the other Protestant, and it was a case of never the two shall meet. We knew which streets not to go down and so did they. It always puzzled me. I had difficulty understanding why schools were segregated by religion. I was forever wondering why people couldn't just get on together.

We appreciated that there was a great deal of animosity between the people of the two religions, but very few of my contemporaries were able to experience different cultures as I did through golf, and indeed that is probably still the case to some extent. Golf allowed me to escape and I quickly found myself in a situation where, travelling throughout Ireland and not just the north, I had far more Catholic friends than Protestant.

This was very much out of the ordinary, but it showed me at an early age just how futile the whole thing was. I know people have their beliefs, but I could never comprehend why it should cost lives and why people could not get on as well as they do in general now. I suppose it's the same throughout the world. It's truly a great shame that a lot of conflict is driven by religion, but the fact is that it's usually a very small percentage of the population who are responsible for the problems. And to me that's a load of nonsense. Looking back, it was crazy what was happening, and I sincerely hope that Northern Ireland never goes back to that again.

My mum's side of the family lost quite a few relations and friends during those dark times and one of the reasons I moved my children to London in the late 1990s was that I didn't want to bring them up in the kind of environment that was the norm in my formative years. I wanted Tyrone and Conor to understand that religion wasn't that big a deal when it came to how you got on with different people; that it was possible to live peacefully among others of different colour, race and creed. They would not have got that perspective in Northern Ireland at that time, but they do now. That's what makes it a much better place in which to live and why I was more than happy to return in 2011.

When my parents took the decision to move to Bushmills, close to where my father was to work at Ballycastle Golf Club on the north coast, it was far less dangerous, but in Dungannon, it was just a way of life . . . and, unfortunately on many an occasion, death.

I remember Dungannon in the early seventies as a very close-knit community and everybody knew one another's business. Few townspeople – roughly 60–40 Catholic to Protestant – were not affected by the problems in one way or another and the golf club and I were no exceptions.

Dungannon Golf Club, founded in 1890, was a regular target during the Troubles and although nobody was ever killed there, it did not enjoy its reputation as the country's most bombed golf club.

My own close call came in 1986 when I was working in one of the bars at Dungannon's Inn On the Park, owned by a couple called Robert and Elaine Watterson, who were very good to me for a long time. I was in from six o'clock that evening, working in the nightclub part of the hotel, setting up the bar, making sure all the glasses and mixers were ready for when the rush started.

We got a bomb-scare phone call at about 9.35 p.m. There were quite a few people in at that stage because drinks were half price up until 10.30. The phoned warning was the same old story we'd heard over and over again, but we always took them seriously because you never knew ... and this time there was a difference.

Usually we'd wait outside until the premises were declared safe, but almost as soon as everybody was outside, the bomb went off – and what a blast there was. It was five to ten and the nightclub was completely flattened. Just twenty minutes after the alert, it disappeared along with half of the hotel. It transpired that the bomb had been in a car just outside the door from five o'clock that afternoon, so I was no more than a few yards away for something like five hours and it could have exploded at any time.

It went off with a fair old bang, but it was nothing new. One thing was certain. I wouldn't be working for the rest of the night, so there was nothing for it but to walk home.

That was one of only two jobs I had before turning professional. The other was in a clothes shop owned by the parents of Gary Johnson, who used to caddie for me. I was one of the shop's best customers as I got everything discounted and I've always been a scratch-handicap shopper. But it was not a job I kept long. I remember giving everybody too much discount.

It wasn't long before golf would take me away from all the Troubles.

3

HOOKED

It was in 1976, when he'd turned 30, that my father discovered golf. He'd tried just about everything else – including cricket, for heaven's sake – when friends took him out one day to Dungannon Golf Club . . . and that was that.

A year or so later, when I was nine, I started caddying for him . . . and that was that for me too. He'd occasionally let me have a putt on the green and whenever one dropped, I'd pick the ball out of the hole and say to myself, 'I think I'm going to enjoy this.' Little did I realise that one day it would not only take me to the pinnacle of the game, but also drive me mental and to the depths of sporting despair.

Some time later, while Dad was enjoying the post-round inquest at the bar, somebody suggested he take up family membership. It would include Mum, Andrea and me, but would only mean an additional £30 or so on the annual fees. So off we all went on a journey that would eventually take me all over the world.

Dad's love affair with the game began with a starter set of Wilson Blue Ridge irons, a driver, four wood and putter. He never really got on with his driver and would use his trusted four wood most of the time. To start with, Mum had never been able to understand why Dad left her at home with me and Andrea every weekend. But after we had been invited to join him on his weekly ritual, the penny as well as the putts started to drop. Mum turned out to be a natural and was firmly hooked after her first visit. Now she's the one who tells people that she leaves my dad at home to go out golfing.

I was immediately fascinated with the game and was encouraged by some kind of natural ability to hit the ball some distance without any tuition or practice with my second-hand set of Wilsons. I stood on the tee, banged away, found the ball, hit it again and that was it. I was hooked.

I was just 11, and only two months after I'd first held a club, I played my first full round with Barry Hamill, who is now a club professional in Northern Ireland. I shot 116 and that included a lot of fresh-air shots, and I counted them all, but I loved every stroke and every minute of it. Ironically, the worse you are, the more you seem to enjoy the game. Amateurs remember their good shots, pros their bad ones.

Golf was instantly the perfect test for me. I'd loved my rugby and team sport, but this was the ultimate. This was me against the course, the unknown, the uncertainty; man against nature. I loved it with an ever-growing passion and I was also extremely comfortable in the surroundings. Dungannon wasn't the old, traditional kind of club. It was more blue collar than silver spoon and it was open to all strata of society. To me it seemed just a normal kind of place, one I could relate to.

I quickly developed heroes. I liked Greg Norman and Seve Ballesteros because of the way they played the game. They took things on and had a go in a cavalier style. That appealed to me more than, say, the way Nick Faldo or Bernhard Langer played. They were wonderful players, but ones who seemed to have a more military strategy to their approach, rather than the colour and flamboyancy of the Australian and Spaniard.

However, I did get something from the Englishman and the German – a sense of style. I acquired an acute taste for nice things long before I could afford them, especially when it came to clothes. I always saved up for the expensive things. I remember when German clothes designer Hugo Boss first launched his collection and they dressed Bernhard Langer. It looked so good I just had to have some, and similarly with Pringle when their model was Nick Faldo. One sweater had his George logo covering almost the entire front and I was a proud wearer. If it was good enough for Bernhard and Nick, then it was definitely good enough for me. I always went for quality over quantity and, although the quantities have also gone up, I'm very much the same today.

Golf quickly became an obsession and there was no containing my enthusiasm or excitement when I slipped my slim bag on my shoulder and travelled the four miles to the course on foot. I'd have walked almost a full round before I reached the club, yet after that trek I'd play another four . . . and if there was any light left, as many holes as I could after that. Seventy-two holes was no particular hardship, particularly for somebody who just smacked the ball, found it and then belted it again without much hesitation.

I could get round comfortably in two hours and I'd play from the moment the sun came up to the second it disappeared. I just couldn't get enough. Before long, I would be standing over putts saying this one is to win the Open, this one for a green jacket, this one for victory at the US Open or PGA. I never aimed below major status. And if I missed, I persisted until I eventually holed one and by then I might be on the fourth hole of a play-off.

Initially, I played a lot with other juniors, like Alistair Cardwell and my cousin Gary Davidson, but I quickly teamed up with older players. I wanted more of a challenge and adults definitely represented that. It wasn't that the other juniors couldn't play, just that I figured if I ever wanted to be any good, then I had to challenge myself against people who were older and better. And that's what I did. My dad felt it would be better if I didn't play so much with him, to take away any pressure, so he fixed me up with two friends of his, Sam Henry and Tommy Lawson. Sammy was a decent amateur and he gave me the basics and a few other tips – and that was me off and running.

There were others I loved playing with, like Hackie, born Raymond McGerr and not nicknamed because of his golf; Paddy Greene; Stanley Stevenson, sadly no longer with us; Brian Smith, who went on to caddie for me a bit; and Boyd Hunter, affectionately known as Floyd. I think it was Dad who once told me that as soon as I got a handicap lower than his, he'd stop playing. He's still out there.

Golf kept me out of trouble. Who knows where I might have found myself if I hadn't discovered this most fascinating and yet frustrating of games? Instead of hanging out with the other kids of my age and getting involved in whatever mischief they might have got into, I was always on the golf course. For me, it was golf, golf, golf, and that's never changed. My manager, Chubby Chandler, has always said that my idea of a day off is a game of golf with mates. He isn't far wrong.

There was a time when I teamed up with three guys from Belfast. They had joined Dungannon because of the expense and lengthy waiting lists of the courses closer to where they lived. We'd play for a couple of quid, and occasionally a tenner if I was feeling lucky. One thing was for certain – however much I played for, I couldn't cover it with what I had in my pocket. That was pressure. Most of the time I didn't embarrass myself, but occasionally I did have to fork out and I hated having to confess that I'd have to pay up later.

Talking of pressure, my four-ball partner Tommy Lawson didn't pitch up one morning when we were due to play a match against players of 10 and 11 handicap, but rather than forfeit, I opted to play our opponents on my own. I was low single figures at the time and the match ended 6&5 to us (me). Those were the days when golf really was fun and I just couldn't get enough.

My handicap came tumbling down and I was off three at 14, when I recorded a net 58 in the first competition I ever won, the Courier Cup. Golf was now in my blood.

4

AMATEUR DAYS

The biggest golfing lessons I received came from my own powers of observation. I can't remember being shown more than the basics by a few friends and my dad. I just watched others and adapted what I'd seen. The first time anybody had the opportunity to give me some tips was when I was selected for the Ulster Boys team.

The coach, former European Tour pro John Garner, saw nothing that needed major surgery. Mind you, if he had I'd probably have taken a second opinion – mine. He told my father that I was the best young golfer he had ever seen and he saw no need to change anything in my swing. He said it would be better to work with what I had rather than try to change it to something that might prove alien and detrimental. Just a few tweaks here and there and I'd be ready to realise my dreams. I only had one – to win the Open Championship.

Those were the only lessons I had, because I didn't feel the need to seek professional advice outside the national set-up at that stage. Things would change. I always believed that it was my destiny to become a professional golfer, and that ambition grew at a fairly fast pace during my teenage years – particularly when my first invitation to do national golf service arrived.

It was a proud day when I pulled on the green jumper and it also pandered to my materialistic tendencies. There was a Golfing Union of Ireland bag, shirts, jumpers and shoes, plus other bits and pieces. But first and foremost, it was a wonderful feeling to be honoured by my country. It was another big step towards my goal.

I was part of the Irish Boys team playing in the Home Internationals of the mid-1980s and although I knew the Irish boys, the ones from England, Scotland and Wales were all new to me. We were playing at Musselburgh, but I can't remember how we got on. I couldn't have done too badly because they kept picking me. In fact, I continued playing for Ireland and Ulster at all levels and then for Great Britain and Ireland in the St Andrews Trophy. But my memories of such events are sketchy. All I was focused on was becoming a professional.

I do remember being trounced by Gary Evans, who was to become a European Tour colleague, in the Amateur Championship and playing against the likes of Sweden's Robert Karlsson and Germany's Sven Strüver, two others I would later regularly come across, but apart from that my biggest recollections are of having a good time, both on and off the course.

I also recall that I was selected to play for Ireland at full international level when I was 16, before Ulster recognised my potential. That was a bit odd. In football terms, it would be like a Liverpool player playing for England before he'd made his Anfield debut. I recently looked at some old photographs from those days and was embarrassed to see that in some I have a big mass of blond hair in a bouffant style. But I wasn't half as embarrassed as my very good friend Eoghan O'Connell the day he discovered that we came from different backgrounds.

I got on well with Eoghan from the moment we met and we would regularly room together as international team-mates. Ireland, as it is with Rugby Union, is one nation when it comes to golf, and because a majority of the tournaments were in the south of the country rather than Ulster, I regularly mixed in mainly Catholic company. In the mid-eighties, most of the boys from the south were either oblivious to what was happening north of the border or too engrossed in their golf to worry about it. Either that or they didn't want to mention it to me, so it was never talked about.

Eoghan, or Farmer as he is affectionately called, was probably oblivious to it all, and we had never discussed it, so he had no idea of my history. On one trip – I think we were in Porthcawl – we were rooming together and on the Sunday morning he jumped out of bed bright and early and shouted across the room, 'Come on, Clarkey.'

I cannot remember my exact response, but it would not have been as polite as 'What on earth are you talking about at this hour?'

'We're going to Mass,' he replied.

'No, I'm not,' I said.

'Yes, you are. It's Sunday and we've got to go to Mass.'

'No, you carry on,' I added.

Then it suddenly dawned on him and you should have seen the look on his face. It was the first time he had roomed with a

Protestant and he wasn't sure what to do. I couldn't help smiling, but, whatever our backgrounds, we are still very good friends to this day and I was honoured to act as his best man.

The first time we met was at the first Boys Home Internationals at Royal St George's and Eoghan was very generous with his praise, although he didn't point out what he considered my faults at the time. He said I was the best ball-striker he had ever seen and he had never seen anybody hit a two iron like I could. Once I learned how to narrow my misses and figure out course management, then the world was my oyster. But his pearls of wisdom did not extend to telling me that I was a mixed talent in that I moved about a lot on my backswing and that I would be prone to excesses of good and bad. It was true. Sometimes you can pure it on the range and do nothing on the course; at other times you can't make contact with the ball in practice but flush it once the gun goes off. Crazy, I know, but that's golf.

In those days, I played every bit as hard as I worked. I definitely subscribed to the view that 'We're only here once'. Even in my early teens, I was travelling all the way round Ireland with the two guys who caddied for me at the time, Brian Smith and Gary Johnson. We'd be on the road for four or five weeks at a time and it certainly accelerated the growing-up process. It gave me an independence which would benefit me greatly. I loved every minute because all I wanted to do was play golf, more golf and then even more golf.

With Mum working as a rep for Imperial Tobacco and both

parents smoking, there was never any shortage of temptation in that department and I succumbed in my mid-teens. It is one of my biggest regrets and the one vice I wish I didn't have. I really wish I hadn't started, because no matter how many times I have tried to stop, I always go back.

Always looking older helped get me into nightclubs and bars and I was as enthusiastic about drinking as I was about smoking. I remember when I was around 16 or 17 my dad taught me a very valuable lesson. He actually allowed me to have more beer than I should have after he'd come to collect me from one night out. On the way home my head started spinning and my stomach erupted all over the back of the car.

I couldn't remember much the following morning, but Dad was ready for me. 'You carry on drinking,' he said. 'You want to be a big boy and get ******, then just carry on. But you will have to clear up the mess afterwards.' And that's what he made me do. I learned my lesson about over-indulgence, although I did continue drinking.

Dad wasn't as understanding the day he came to fetch me after a week's competition in Galway at an Irish Boys tournament. They'd given me £400 to cover food and lodgings, plus the usual blank cheque in case of emergencies, but I had arranged to stay in a tent to save money.

I did reasonably well in the golf and enjoyed myself as much as I could off the course as well. Galway is a great place to have a good time because it has wonderful watering holes and every-thing else a young lad with a few bob in his pocket might need.

But very soon I had a lot more than a few bob after a friend of mine found an amusement arcade with a poker machine that was spitting out winning cards nine times out of ten. Before long we had accumulated more than £1,500 between us.

Young lads with cash and no great desire to hang on to it proved a big magnet and we had no difficulty finding new friends who were more than happy to join us in having a good time. So we'd play golf, buy drinks, smoke and enjoy ourselves, before starting the process all over again. Beer, fags and some new clothes meant that I went through my cash faster than I realised and my generosity eventually caught up with me. My £400 expenses plus £750 from the poker machine disappeared faster than a tap-in.

I got knocked out in the third round and called home to ask Dad to come and collect me, but he arrived earlier than I expected, discovered that I was staying in a tent and opened the flaps to find me entertaining a new-found friend.

Dad bundled me into the car and verbally laid into me all the way home. His mood did not improve when I told him that not only had I spent all my money, but I had also cashed in the blank cheque for another £400. Nothing much has changed since then – spending money, I mean, not sharing tents with girls.

I was always determined to turn professional, but just how my golfing future was going to take shape, I wasn't entirely sure. So when Eoghan went to take up a place at Wake Forest University, one of America's foremost golfing nurseries, which had nurtured

Arnold Palmer, Curtis Strange, Lanny Wadkins and more recently Bill Haas and Webb Simpson, it seemed a logical step to follow in his wake, so to speak.

Kids turn professional much earlier these days, particularly outside America, but back in my day the preferred route was through the American collegiate system, so that's the way I went. I sat and passed the SAT examinations in Dublin, then packed my bags in search of an American dream, fuelled by my enthusiasm and some help from a Dungannon-based company called Powerscreen. Little did I imagine that it would quickly turn into a nightmare.

I loved Wake Forest, thought it was a wonderful place, and was looking forward to my next few years in America when I arrived in January 1989. Under the NCAA rules, you are only allowed to play for the university for four years, starting in September, so from January to August I just practised and studied . . . and was introduced to a linebacker from the football squad, or at least he introduced himself to me.

The guy was substantially bigger than I was and he accused me of having chatted up his girlfriend. I'm not sure whether I had or not, but whatever the case, I wasn't going to be intimidated, so I leant into him and asked what he was going to do about it. Looking back at the disparity in size at the time, it's probably a good job that he opted not to take the matter any further. It would not be the last occasion that I stood my ground at Wake Forest, and the next time would have far more serious consequences.

On returning from the summer break, I'm fairly sure I led

qualifying for the team and I was disappointed not to be selected by legendary coach Jesse Haddock for the number one-ranked side. Two weeks later, I coasted through the second qualifier, yet I still wasn't selected. This time I was not disappointed. I was angry.

I've never been frightened of fronting up and, in my opinion, my lack of selection was at least worthy of an explanation. I went into the office for a discussion with Mr Haddock. The discussion turned into a heated discussion. The heated discussion turned into an argument and the argument turned into me telling coach Haddock where he could stick his scholarship. I packed my bags and left the campus, never to return.

It seemed that there was only one way to do things in Wake Forest's golf programme and that was Mr Haddock's way. His way or the highway, and I chose the highway. Apparently, he wasn't used to scholars who drank and smoked, even though I never got into trouble, went to all the classes, got decent grades and put all my hours in on the range.

I just didn't know what was going on with Mr Haddock, so we never saw eye to eye. If I think I'm out of order, I'll hold my hands up. If I don't think I'm out of order, I'll stand my ground. I've always been that way, rightly or wrongly. In this case, I didn't think I was doing anything wrong, so I stood my ground and he stood his ground and we parted ways, never to tread the same ground again . . . at least not until I met him at Augusta some years later.

The Wake Forest alumni were having something of a

get-together at the Masters and when he spotted me, he walked over, put his arms around me and said, 'No hard feelings, Darren. I always knew you were going to do OK.' That surprised me because I'm not sure he ever saw me hit a shot when I was at Wake Forest. I just looked at him, smiled and muttered something I can't remember, but I think he got my drift.

I wasn't the only angry person when I cut short my American university scholarship. My dad was far from delighted that his only son was heading home so soon after leaving. So much so that he refused to collect me from the airport. It was a task he was more than happy to leave to Mum, although he would have his say later.

Mum did not hold back either. No sooner had the car door closed as we headed out of the airport than she told me that the whole family were disappointed at my decision to return, not just Dad. I could understand it from their perspective because of the sacrifices they had all made. But the row I'd had with the coach meant that nothing was ever going to work there after that, so I didn't have an option.

Dad's way of thinking was that I'd been given a wonderful opportunity and had thrown it away. Well, I didn't see it that way and they already knew just how headstrong I was. You have to be a bit like that in golf and I hadn't gone to America not to play on the team, and if I wasn't playing competitively it was a big waste of time being there. As far as I was concerned, my position was untenable because I'd qualified for the team yet the coach had refused to select me.

It was my decision to quit and I still think it was the right one, although I understood where my parents were coming from when they criticised and questioned my actions. Although they had a busy social life and loved to enjoy themselves, they had sacrificed so much for me, as had Andrea. Every spare penny they earned went on me and my golf.

There was no going back and they realised it, but they had every right to point out what they had done to help me follow my dreams. Now I not only had to prove to them that I had made the right decision in returning, but also to myself.

5

TURNING PRO

The pressure was on at the start of 1990, but I have always enjoyed being at the sharp end and gradually things would turn in my favour.

Within a year the wins started and kept on coming. I won the Spanish Amateur and followed that with the North of Ireland, the South of Ireland and the Irish Amateur Close Championship. The Wake Forest misadventure was long forgotten.

Now I was in a position to determine my own future, but people expected me to wait until after the Walker Cup in September 1991, which was to be staged at Portmarnock, one of my favourite courses, before turning professional. Staying amateur had its attractions, not least playing in one of team golf's oldest and most distinguished amateur events. In those days, it also guaranteed a few starts if you did turn professional fairly soon afterwards. So there were some pros in not turning pro.

I debated with myself for a long time. I'd had a great year and the Walker Cup was still some way off. I probably wouldn't top what I'd just done if I waited, so really all I was doing was killing time for the kudos of putting Walker Cup on my CV. In the meantime, winning the Irish Close had also had an added bonus in that it got me into the Irish Open, where I was delighted to be paired with Sam Torrance for the first two rounds. If I had had any doubts about turning professional, and when to do it, Sam quickly dispelled them. There was no time like the present, was his advice. Very soon I would be taking it.

I'd thought about turning pro even before I won the Spanish Amateur. It was at that stage, in the February of 1990, that my good friend and solicitor in Dungannon, Fergie Patton, wanted to have a chat and asked what my intentions were. I said I wanted to turn pro and he said to leave it to him.

Fergie called a certain world-renowned sports management company and told them he knew this young guy who was intending to turn pro and would they be interested in looking after him. He didn't hear a peep back, not even a courtesy call, so we just left it and didn't get in touch with them again.

Later in the year, while I was winning everything and just before the Irish Close Championship in Baltray, the press asked me what I was going to do. Would I stay amateur and play the Eisenhower Trophy – I had a good chance of making the four-man Great Britain and Ireland team – or was I going down the professional route?

I said I wasn't sure, but I wasn't naive enough to think I could just jump the amateur ship without having a management set-up behind me, and the one we'd contacted hadn't seemed that interested.

It was then that another friend, Dublin lawyer Dougie Heather, a former Irish international amateur golfer, got in touch and said that a friend of his in England, Chubby Chandler, had just started a management company and would I be interested in chatting to him? I was, so Dougie phoned Chubby and told him about me and that I might be good for his stable.

Chubby was definitely interested in talking to me, so Dougie advised him to get to Dublin as soon as he could because I was going to win the Irish on Sunday. Dougie obviously had every confidence in me, and it was not ill-founded, because I promptly went out and won it – beating Padraig Harrington in the final.

The following morning I went to meet Chubby in Dougie's office and the Lancastrian was as gregarious then as he is now, but slightly slimmer – although the same could be said of me.

The meeting wasn't specifically about Chubby managing me, just him offering advice about turning professional, what I would have to do and the various bits and bobs associated with the change of codes. I remember his main piece of advice was that I'd be better off turning professional straight away than waiting another year. His argument was that professionals worked harder and I would definitely be a better player in a year than I would if I stayed amateur.

He also said that even if I waited for the Walker Cup there would be no guarantees of contracts or playing invitations. We talked for about an hour, and the more I heard, the more I realised that not only was I ready to turn pro, I also wanted Chubby to be my manager.

We had a full and all-embracing meeting and my bottom line was: 'Look after my finances and everything else, because all I want to do and can be bothered to do is play golf.' Little did he know the hassle he was going to have with me over the years, but we shook hands and that was it, apart from one thing. Chubby said he did not know a great deal about cars, so could I look after that aspect of our arrangement? I was more than happy to do so.

I'd asked Chubby about a contract and he said that when Arnold Palmer and lawyer Mark McCormack, whose IMG agency would become world-renowned, first started their association they shook hands on the deal and stayed like that throughout their careers. If it was good enough for them, then it was certainly good enough for me.

Meanwhile, in the London offices of a certain management company, somebody had obviously been scanning the newspapers and discovered that I was about to turn professional. Miraculously, after six months, they had even found Fergie Patton's telephone number and called several times, saying that they would like to speak to me.

Fergie managed to get hold of me just as I was coming out of the meeting with Chubby and he told me that this company were now keen to speak with me. I told Fergie that I had just signed, or shaken hands rather, with Chubby and he should tell them that I was joining International Sports Management. It was a decision I was very happy with and have never regretted.

Fergie called the world-renowned management company back and told a certain person what had just happened and that if he wanted any more information he should call Chubby Chandler. The agent, who I don't think works for the company now, said,

'You can tell that young Mr Clarke he has just made the biggest mistake of his career,' and then hung up. These days I have great delight running into the guy.

I was ready to go. Now it was time to test myself in a couple of little pro-ams just to get into the swing of things before heading to Tour School . . . the road to dreams.

6

STEPHEN BOLER

I had my first foot on the ladder, but I had a lot to learn about golf and life before I would be climbing at any pace. Much of that education came at Mere Golf and Country Club in Cheshire. It was more to me than just a golfing oasis and the home of International Sports Management. Its owner, Stephen Boler, became an influential character in my life.

Boler, before his very untimely death, was an entrepreneur who started out as a 16-year-old trainee with Unilever in Sierra Leone. He made his first fortune selling tyres and exhausts at cut price and went on to buy Mere in 1983. At one point, he was the largest single shareholder in Manchester City – how he would have loved the 2011–12 season – and went on to become a leader in conservation in South Africa, creating the Tswalu game reserve in the Kalahari.

Stephen was unbelievably generous towards me and taught me much about life matters, fly fishing and fine red wine. His knowledge of the grape had come, as would mine, through drinking it as much as reading about it. There was an immediate chemistry between us when we met in the early 1990s and that continued until his premature death of a heart attack at the age of just 55.

I first knew of Mere through Chubby's attachment to it as a professional and it became his base when he formed ISM in 1989 on the back of a $10,000 overdraft from the bank. Yes, he was that rich.

Chubby has always operated on a system based on first impressions and he has been right far more than the opposite. So when the girl he employed to be his assistant asked him on the first day, 'When am I going to meet the boys, then?', he decided he would not be fielding any more questions from her and sent her out of the door faster than she'd opened it.

It was then that Chubby turned to a very good amateur golfer called Debbie Howard, who had been working for the PGA Northern Region in their little office at Mere. When the PGA moved to Bolton Golf Club, she then worked for the Ladies European Tour at Tytherington, Cheshire, but knew Chubby socially through Mere, while her mum, Ann, also knew him through playing for Lancashire Ladies when he'd played for Lancashire Boys.

When Chubby asked her to work for him, she accepted and immediately moved back into the same office she'd previously worked in at Mere. Debbie is a wonderful girl with a great sense of humour and is now happily married to my good friend and European Tour colleague Richard Finch, but back then she had her moments – every Monday, in fact. To this day I never call her on a Monday because of the memories of when she'd snap and snarl at anybody who had the audacity to ring the office while she was working out commissions and VAT. Grumpy doesn't do her Monday attitude justice.

Debbie also fielded weekly calls from my bank manager, because I have to admit I never have been good with money and today nothing much has changed. He would ring every Monday morning without fail asking if there was any likelihood of funds being deposited. He said he would much prefer it if I banked with them rather than them banking with me.

I got on instantly with Debbie. She was my go-to girl, doing the bookings and reservations, and would frequently give me a rollicking for overspending. It was also Debbie who was sent to shepherd me through Tour School in Montpellier. Now, Debbie has many talents, but back then one of them was definitely not cooking. We were sharing an apartment and there weren't many restaurants nearby, so she decided to boil a chicken. It didn't go well. I think we went hungry that night.

A few days later we weren't eating again, but this time it was because we were drinking to celebrate me graduating Tour School. It hadn't been looking too promising coming towards the end of a long week, but a four-under-par 32 on the back nine of the last round saw me scrape through to collect one of the last cards available. Thankfully, I would never have to return.

After I'd completed the six-round marathon, she found me in a bar staring into what she described as an enormous bowl of lager. A few of these later and she struggled to get me into and out of the car as, with all the excitement and adrenalin, I quickly got absolutely slaughtered.

Debbie also accompanied me, Marcus Wills and James Berry to South Africa in 1991. One Sunday we ended up in a nightclub in Johannesburg, but when we came out, there were no taxis around, so Debbie toured the area and eventually begged a lift for us all from a farmer who was towing a horsebox. We jumped in the back and were dropped off in Sandton, safely home although covered in straw and smelling of you-know-what. Happy days.

Debbie was devoted to helping Chubby in his new career. I was his first young client and he saw me as his chance to really kick-start the company. Its subsequent progress owed no small thanks to Debbie. In early 1991, she started going out with SEB, as she affectionately referred to Stephen Boler, and a year later was too busy to continue working for Chubby, though she never lost touch.

I went over to Mere the week after I had shaken hands with Chubby on our working relationship. He had only recently retired from the European Tour after a long career which had seen him win the São Paulo Open and end up owing the bank money. He still knew which end of the club to hold and we had a good match on that first visit, even though he negotiated a few more shots than he should have received. He would later tell me that after we played he went home that night and said to himself, 'I've now got a business. This is my big opportunity.'

Chubby told me he had only ever been intimidated a couple of times on a golf course by somebody's hitting. The first time it was Sandy Lyle, who had thrown his ball on the ground, pulled out a one iron and promptly smashed it past his driver with his shirt flapping in the breeze. Then there was Seve, because he was Seve . . . and now me. He had been really impressed by what he referred to as my 'towering three irons'.

My increasingly frequent visits to Mere were always fun. I'd come over for the weekend and play with Chubby and Boler and their friends – anything up to twelve guys, all playing a match against one another for maybe £50 – far more than I'd been used to playing for.

It was the first time I really came across a bit of hustling and gamesmanship. Just before I was about to hit, I would be reminded where it would be advisable to avoid, where there was water and out of bounds. These were not golf games, just mind games, and I became mentally tougher because of them, although I wasn't so appreciative at the time. That was the style and the general atmosphere. But it made me stronger.

After we'd played, we'd go into the clubhouse and check our cards against everybody else's to see where the money was apportioned. There would be guys like Stephen's son Mark, Bob Dugdale, John Griffin, Mike Hazeldene, Alan Brindle, Les Hampson, Peter Smith and the late Max Brown and Ian Blenkinsop all frantically checking their cards in the clubhouse as we played matches from everybody's scores on every hole.

When it came to Boler, there was always a bit of friendly mischief. I'd say I'd had a four on the first and he'd say he'd had a five, so I was one up; then I might say I'd had a four and he'd say three, all square. But it was when I said a number and he said 'similar' to get a half that you knew he'd either lost a ball or gone

49

in the water and forgotten to count the penalties. He tried to get away with it as many times as he could, and because he owned the place no one stood up to him.

Occasionally, when I'd got a couple of grand credit up on him, I said, 'When are you ever going to pay me?' Boler would invariably have the last word, because he'd just turn and say, 'Put it down to aviation fuel.' He was shocking, but it was always done in a fun way and I always let him get away with it. Boler loved taking the mick and I was never slow to respond. We spent many a long night decanting a glass of red or three into our stomachs, telling stories and having fun.

The fuel line was something you could never argue with, because Boler was always very generous with his private plane and helicopter. He was friendly with all Chubby's clients, playing golf and tennis with us and taking us fishing on the River Helmsdale in the Highlands, usually the week after the Open. It was there that I caught my first salmon and began my love of fly fishing.

It was all good banter at Mere, and excellent at toughening me up for what was to come on the world's circuits, particularly as they always haggled for more shots than they should be receiving. Bob, who was off six at the time, did this one day and I had to write him a rather large cheque. It made me realise that if I was to survive, then I'd have to get into the swing of the gamesmanship business and start handing it out myself. It was all part of the fun of playing with these guys. I learnt a lot from those days at Mere.

My life lessons from Boler ended way too soon, however. His death from a heart attack affected me deeply because we had been such good friends. He was heading for his game reserve with Debbie in his Falcon 900, but felt unwell on landing and decided to head straight back to Johannesburg. The paramedics came on board at Lanseria Airport, but he was pronounced dead before arriving at the hospital.

Boler died two days before the start of the Volvo Masters in 1998 and Chubby was not quite sure whether to tell me or not because there was a lot at stake in Jerez, not least the Order of Merit title. He knew I would be hit hard by the news, but eventually he thought he'd better tell me rather than risk me hearing it from somebody else.

'Go out and win it for Boler,' he said.

I did, and I dedicated the win to him in a tough acceptance speech.

Chubby kindly came to Debbie's rescue and kept her busy travelling around the UK organising the Business Golf Championship with Les Massey, also formerly of PGA North Region, before she was hit with another massive blow. In 2003, she was diagnosed with something I was way too familiar with, breast cancer. Heather spent many hours on the phone going through everything with her about chemo and radiotherapy. Because she couldn't travel as much, Chubby gave her the job of looking after the ISM websites . . . from her sick bed. This included mine and she still runs it to this day.

7

SOUTH AFRICA

I didn't have an abundance of self-confidence when I first went into the professional ranks in 1990, but enough to be thinking I wasn't out of place or out of my depth. My attitude and work ethic is the same today as it was then. I have never been able to accept playing poorly, because that's not why I am on the road. Whatever other people have thought, said and written, there has never been a critic who has come anywhere near how tough I am on myself, but I've never been frightened to get my head down and keep working, working, working.

My fiery temperament has been somewhat dampened with age, but I can still get angry with myself very quickly if I play anything less than half decent. It's a facet of my personality which has driven me on but also contributed to periods of being down in the dumps.

I was still very bright-eyed in the early months of 1991. There wasn't much happening in Europe at that time of year, so Chubby packed me off to South Africa and the beginning of a long love affair with the continent. Chubby's friends there, including Johann Rupert, the Mr Big of South African sport, and Selwyn Nathan, now Sunshine Tour commissioner, became friends and remain so to this day.

Louis Martin, another friend of Chubby's who would become chief executive of the tour there and then the Asia circuit, was given the task of looking after me as I started out on my professional career with what Chubby described as a flamboyant dress sense, flamboyant hairstyle and a flamboyant style of play.

I thoroughly enjoyed myself in South Africa, didn't really get into contention, but cut my teeth there and felt ready for whatever I might face anywhere and everywhere.

The attraction of South Africa was instant – great golf courses with people to match: Des Terblanche, Fulton Allem, Ernie Els, Retief Goosen, David Frost, Nick Price, Mark McNulty and many more including my all-time swing hero Simon Hobday. What a vast amount of talent I was able to tap into purely through playing with them and socialising – both activities South Africans have always been good at.

I want to single out Simon Hobday, however, because he is as mad as a hatter, something I can relate to. I am fortunate to have been in his company, because he is a storyteller extraordinaire . . . and what a swing. It's simply the best you could possibly have.

As for Nick Price, you couldn't meet a nicer gentleman in the world of golf. Not all are as they appear, but Pricey is. He's as genuine as it gets. The way he strikes a golf ball and the way he swings – everything about him is just quality. And talking about swings, they don't come any more rhythmical than the Big Easy. The nickname is something of a misnomer, however, because although he comes across as laid-back, few work harder at their game than Ernie Els.

There are plenty of South Africans in my little black book – the one I keep detailing all the tips and bits of advice I have received over the years. David Frost features prominently for putting, because he's been one of the best ever, and I have contributions from all the greats of my time – Seve, Greg, Vijay Singh, anybody who has hit a shot I wanted to know how to do, have all been included.

I don't know which of the South Africans it was who taught me a few words of Afrikaans but none can be translated without the use of many asterisks. The people and the country have always been very kind to me – not least Dimension Data, who sponsored me for a while. They were and still are very generous and always thanked me for supporting their tour. I'll never forget the helping hand they gave me and that's one of the reasons I keep going back.

South Africa is also one of the few places where I have been fined during my career. I was with Lee Westwood and Chubby and we decided to have a practice round on the Lost City course prior to the Million Dollar Challenge. Unbeknown to us, we were breaking Tour rules by riding in buggies. A few of the elder statesmen on the Sunshine Tour spotted us and the word quickly got back to tour head Louis Martin. He was accused of indulging his British friends, but Louis knew nothing of it and asked head rules guy Theo Manyama to look into it.

Theo found us and said he would have to fine us 250 rand – the equivalent of about £10. We said OK, but can we finish off our round in the carts to get our money's worth, and he said that was all right as long as we paid the fine afterwards. I'm not sure if we ever paid, but if we did, it would have been with pleasure.

One story from South Africa, however, does not actually involve anybody from that country but my Ryder Cup colleague and former Sunningdale neighbour Paul McGinley. We were playing in Johannesburg and rooming together in Sandton when one night Paul poked me in the ribs and said, 'D, D, D, wake up, there's a bird in the room.'

He was referring to one of the feathered variety and I told him he was talking rubbish and to go back to sleep. He persisted with his claims and frantically searched the room to find it, but to no avail. It took him fifteen minutes to realise that the bird noise was actually me grinding my teeth.

One person who didn't see the funny side of some Darren Clarke noises was Louis Martin, when he was the Sunshine Tour's commissioner.

At the time I used to stay with him, I was very well looked after by his attractive daughter Kim, who was 15 but looked older. She was always great company and made sure everything was sorted. Louis was extremely proud of her and quite rightly.

On one visit we were by the pool just before it was time for me to return to Europe and I told her that I was going to wind her father up when he came home by telling him I was going to take her out for dinner.

As soon as Louis walked in I said to him, 'Listen, I need to talk to you, so sit down. You know how kind you and Kim have been and everything's been great and wonderful and I'll see you again shortly, but as a thank you I'd like to take your daughter out to dinner.'

I could see the blood drain from Louis's face and his reply could not have been louder had he used a loudhailer at point-blank range. 'ABSOLUTELY NOT' was the gist of his expletive-riddled and emphatic response.

'Steady on, Louis,' I replied as he continued in the same vein. 'I don't mean anything untoward to your daughter, but she's been very good to me and I'd like to take her out as a thank you.'

It was just as Louis was about to burst another blood vessel that I disappeared to my room. Having known what Louis's reaction would be, I'd rehearsed this bit with Kim and told her that when she heard me going to my room, she should come out and also ask her father.

Kim came bounding through and said, 'Dad, I have a favour to ask. Darren wants to take me out to dinner. It's OK, isn't it?'

Louis went absolutely potty with Kim too and it was brilliant to behold. We had him hook, line and sinker and it was quite some time before he began to see the funny side of our little trick. And to this day we still wind him up about it.

I left the country still smiling and in the knowledge that South Africans were very much like the Irish golfers in loving their sport and enjoying themselves at the same time. I always look forward to my trips there.

8

WINNING WAYS

Armed with a Titleist deal and the backing of Christchurch Insurance Brokers, in 1991 I was ready to pit myself against Europe's best after enjoying my time in South Africa.

I wasn't short of travelling, practising and socialising colleagues. It's only natural for cliques to exist when you have a weekly travelling group of 150 or so players and caddies. Such is the nature of the European Tour that it draws players from every continent. Consequently Irish, English, Scots, Spanish, Swedish, people from the Far East, Australasia, South Americans and the occasional American gravitate towards their own kind. And even though I had my own ISM 'minders', there were always a fair few Irish, and it was towards those that I would drift, particularly after the last practice shot had been hit.

The older Irish guys used to try to look after the new kids. They showed us the ropes and introduced us to life on the Tour with all its banter and practical jokes. It was a toughening-up process. We were a varied crew in the nicest possible way and there was always plenty of laughter. Philip Walton was usually the ringleader when it came to a bit of friendly mischief and I remember acting as lookout one day when he decided that Eamonn Darcy had a much-too-posh new suitcase. Darce had left the room briefly and before he re-emerged Walts produced some superglue from his pocket and squeezed it into the locks. The only way it could be opened was to cut into it, and so the suitcase made just one trip before it went into the bin. Its replacement was not quite so expensive.

Nobody took more stick than legendary Irish caddie John O'Reilly, who on one occasion found his case half full of clothes and the other half water, while on another he made the schoolboy error of leaving the table with food still on his plate. By the time he returned it had an added ingredient he was not aware of until it was in his stomach. Red-hot chilli peppers can test even the strongest constitution. This was Boys on Tour.

Although I loved playing golf with the Irish boys, there were others I was always more than happy to accompany on to the tee. Ian Woosnam was a particular favourite because he was so natural and flushed it, and I always enjoyed being paired with Sam Torrance, a real pro's pro. It was invariably fun with them and it was all part of the learning curve.

Chubby's ethos was similar to that of the Irish lads – the older guys in his stable looked after the new kids on the tee. That's always been one of the most endearing qualities of ISM, and it's still how it works today. At the time, Chubby had about five clients and three of them – Carl Mason, now winning for fun on the Seniors Tour; Richard Boxall, now operating behind Sky golf microphones; and mutual friend Derek Cooper – were given the job of indoctrinating me into the ways of the Tour. Mace was the senior minder and would always ensure I had a partner for practice or dinner. There was always somebody keeping an eye on me and I was grateful for all the help, encouragement and advice I received in my formative Tour years.

When we practised we'd always play for cash, although bragging rights were far more important. We only played for a few quid, though, not silly money. I have always been pleased that I never really got into horse racing and gambling, because with my nature I'd have put on so much money that it would have hurt had I lost. I never saw the point in doing that. I don't know how to go into a bookmakers and fill out a betting slip, but that's deliberate, because with my compulsive nature it would be far too dangerous. Don't get me wrong, I have a bet now and again on a horse or football if I get a tip. But some years ago I learned a very expensive lesson.

I was in Japan – great country, love the food and Tokyo – playing at the Chunichi Crowns in Nagoya and at a loss for what to do, given that I'd done all the practice I could and there wasn't a great deal of obvious entertainment in the area. I decided to go back to my hotel and rest a bit because I was still coping with a slight case of jet lag. What possessed me, I have no idea, but I went online and started playing blackjack. I was merrily clicking away and within half an hour I'd lost £20,000.

If my fingers had been burned any more I would have had to send for the fire brigade. This was in the late 1990s and the early years of online gambling, and I'd just wasted a shedload of money. I immediately said to myself, 'What are you doing? You're just throwing your money away.' In one way it was pathetic and stupid, but in another it taught me a lesson. I'm so glad I didn't win that first time. I've never done it again.

I'll never forget my first Tour cheque. It is as memorable as the biggest, and mine came from finishing 29th in the Girona Open in 1991. I received the princely sum of £2,000 and I'm not certain what happened to it. One thing is for sure, I would have spent every last penny.

A player's first year on the Tour is the big one in terms of ensuring you keep your card and mine in the 1991 season wasn't secure until very late in the year. I eventually finished 112th in the Order of Merit, earning £30,000 from eleven events, including one top ten and having missed the cut in eight events.

Even though I was way down the list, I did feel as if I belonged and was quietly confident that I was heading in the right direction. That became fact in 1992, my second season, when I had one runner-up finish, at the Honda Open in Hamburg, and ended the year 41st on the money list, having had five other top tens, grossing £140,000. I also had my first serious chance of winning a tournament that year, when I held a five-shot lead at the European Monte Carlo Open after firing the first of my two Tour 60s in the second round.

Chubby was on holiday in Portugal at the time, but he flew from Faro to Nice and then got a cab up the coast to Mont Agel. His words were very encouraging. 'You're on your own today,' he said. 'I never had a five-shot lead in my career so I'm not sure what to tell you.' I ended up being pipped by Ian Woosnam, finishing in fourth place, but it was great experience and I was getting nearer.

I did win the 1992 Ulster Professional Championship, but the big European Tour breakthrough came in 1993, which saw me amass a then mind-blowing £370,000 and brought my first win, at the **Alfred Dunhill Belgian Open** at Royal Zoute in Knokke, which accounted for £100,000 of the season's earnings.

It wasn't so much the cash that impressed me as the names on the leader board and further down the field. Behind me was a veritable who's who of not just European but world golf. The final leader board read:

1 Clarke
2= Faldo
2= Singh
4= Ballesteros
4= Langer

And further down the list were such names as Torrance, Rocca, Frost, Woosnam, Karlsson, Els and Montgomerie.

At the start of the final day, I was obviously very nervous but my focus was great. This was what I wanted to do, why I practised so hard. I was finally in the position that all those long and lonely hours hitting balls had steered me towards. And I really wanted that first win, which gets harder to achieve the longer it eludes you.

I was in elite company and played the last round alongside my boyhood hero, Seve. What an experience that proved to be. This was Seve the legend, an intimidating figure, but my days with the Mere boys had toughened me up for anything I might encounter against professionals, who are far more subtle when it comes to playing mind games.

I held a slender lead standing on the 17th tee and we both laid up on the par five. It was Seve at his best, because I was about 140 yards out and he was some 30 yards closer. It was my shot, but Seve walked straight down the middle of the fairway to the green and back again while I was still waiting. It was classic Seve, obviously testing the rookie, but I managed to hold on and win by two shots. What a very good tournament and field for a maiden victory.

Chubby came out for the final day having driven down from Manchester to Dover in the pride of his life, a Toyota Supra, staying the night in a Premier Inn, catching the first ferry and then driving up the coast. We had breakfast and then he followed me on my most important eighteen holes to date. When he said he was driving back, I opted to join him, stuffing my luggage on the back seat with the trophy sitting proudly but uneasily on top – alongside the flag from the 18th green. It had been Chubby's greatest day as a manager to that point and it was to get even better within twenty-four hours.

The following morning I flew to Belfast while Chubby continued his way back north in the Supra, continually pressing the overdrive button, which he was obsessed by. Chubby was in his office by 3 p.m. and within an hour he took a call from a man who said his son was about to turn pro, had already spoken to a few management companies and would he be interested in talking to him? He'd seen how I'd been managed. Chubby drove over to John Westwood's house and very soon afterwards he had a new, young and promising talent to manage ... and I had both a friendly rival and a new friend.

Chubby often gave us advice about anything and everything, not just golf. One year he was flying with me to the World Cup in Puerto Rico and we were on Delta and in First Class. I was wearing jeans, T-shirt and trainers, as were Mark McNulty and Tony Johnstone, who were representing Zimbabwe. Ian Woosnam was also on board and looking very smart, wearing grey slacks and shoes and a cashmere jumper. Chubby just turned to me and said, 'Who's the US Masters champion on here?' I could see what he meant about Ian and it was a lesson I have never forgotten. Whenever Lee and I go to an official function, we're up there among the best dressed. If we have the choice of wearing a suit or not, we'll wear a suit.

It was a message I was happy to pass on. Many years later I travelled on the same plane to Thailand as ISM colleague Simon Dyson and he was carrying a suit cover. I asked him why he had a suit with him and he said, 'You never know, I might need one.'

Sure enough, Simon was invited to a function and when we got there he, Lee and I were the only ones wearing suits. 'Well done, Dys. You look great,' I told him. 'You'll find you can never overdress. Chubby told me that years ago.'

Meanwhile, let me take you back to the aftermath of my win in the Alfred Dunhill Belgian Open. I had still not taken possession of my new, or should I say second-hand, toy. Before the tournament, I'd treated myself to an 18-month-old Porsche 911 Carrera, my first but far from last of that particular brand, and I was very much looking forward to driving it on my return. I had it for five minutes.

I'd bought the car privately, but when I got home I looked at the winner's cheque and decided that I'd go all the way and get a new one, trading in the car I'd just bought, although I kept the number plate – C911 YES.

In 1994, I added the Irish PGA Championship to my CV, but it would take me two more years before my second European Tour win. I shook off a determined Mark Davis and Paul Broadhurst to win the 1996 **Linde German Masters** by one shot. I did most of my damage on the front nine of the final round when I birdied the second, chipped in for eagle on the fourth, birdied the fifth and added more at the seventh, eighth and ninth.

A three-shot win in the **Benson & Hedges International Open** in 1998 was followed by success at the season-ending **Volvo Masters** in Jerez. It was my biggest win so far, but it was a triumph filled with sadness because of the news of Stephen Boler's sudden and totally unexpected death. I played some of the time in a daze, but I followed Chubby's instructions to the letter by winning it for him. I did it with a course record-equalling 63 in the last round, coming from three behind to pip my by then ISM stablemate Andrew Coltart by two shots, with Colin Montgomerie third – a high enough position for the Scot to collect another

Order of Merit title, with me in second place, something I have achieved on two more occasions.

Jerez was also Tyrone's introduction to the media; he'd been born that year and Heather and he came out for pictures with the trophy on the last green. But it was still something of a tense situation, because Boler should have been there and he'd have said, 'Well done, Bog Trotter', for that was his nickname for me. He's still sadly missed.

The 1999 season was memorable in another way in that I came within a whisker of being disqualified from the Volvo Masters at Montecastillo in the most bizarre circumstances. The clock was ticking ever closer to tee time and I was locked in the toilet.

Most players go to the bathroom before starting a round and I was availing myself of the opportunity in one of the three traps. But when I went to open the door, something had jammed and my cries for help were not being answered. Eventually, my caddie, Billy Foster, came in to find out where I was and tried to kick down the door, but without immediate success. There was only one thing to do – climb over the eight-foot high concrete wall into the next cubicle.

It wasn't until I started getting over the top that I realised there was somebody in there with unfinished business. He said something in Spanish. I apologised, dropped down and then made it out of the door in the nick of time.

But my favourite story revolves around a similar situation in Augusta, when one of the British press corps found himself having a dialogue with an unknown colleague using the only other cubicle in the bathroom.

'Excuse me, but would you mind passing me a few sheets of paper,' said a voice in distress.

'Unfortunately I can't, because there's no more left in here,' came the reply.

'Oh, no,' said the guy. 'How about a newspaper?'

'Sorry, there isn't one.'

There was a short silence and then the man made one final plea. 'Do you have two fives for a ten?'

It wasn't much longer before my fifth European Tour title arrived and with it my love affair with the **English Open**, which would see me win three of them in four years – the first at Hanbury Manor in 1999.

The most memorable thing of that week was that in both the second and third rounds, I finished with five straight birdies. I eventually finished just two shots ahead of John Bickerton, having moved to seven clear at the first when I holed a bunker shot.

If I enjoyed Hanbury Manor, I was to like the Forest of Arden outside Birmingham even more when the English Open moved there the following year. It was somewhat strange that I immediately liked the course, because it was only a few miles down the road from the Belfry, where I've never really played that well in a tournament – although I did enjoy a little success there at the Ryder Cup. The Forest of Arden was different and I won there twice in three years.

It helps massively when you like a course. You see shots so much more easily. When players say a course fits their eye, it basically means they like a certain hole and the shape of the shot that some holes dictate. It's one of the main reasons why some guys play well on some courses and some don't. The Forest of Arden fitted my eye perfectly.

I've always been a bit of a tinkerer when it comes to my clubs, but what happened during my second **English Open** win, in 2000, was bizarre even by my standards. I used the clubs I'd practised with for the first round, changed to another set for the second and another for the third, and then went back to the ones from round one. I'm not sure why I did it; I must have thought it was a good idea at the time. Nobody else in the world would have been stupid enough to have even tried that. I won it despite myself. And I did it in quite some style – shooting 65 in the last round, with ten birdies, including four in succession from the 13th to overcome a six-shot deficit and win by one, with Michael Campbell second and Mark James third.

Golf has rarely reduced me to tears, but there were a few at the K Club in County Kildare in 1999 . . . induced by Lee Westwood among other things. It was the last round of the European Open and I was preparing at one end of the range while Lee was at the other.

Chubby remembers Lee having a cheeky look in his eye; he was seven back and saying that if he got off to a quick start it might make life interesting. I was working with sports psychologist

Jos Vanstiphout at the time and I remember Chubby telling me afterwards that when he'd expected to see calmness and peace, what he saw was anything but. Jos was on the putting green poking me in the ribs, as was his style, winding me up as if it was a heavyweight title fight.

Lee got his wish, because he was three under after four, so my overnight lead had been cut, and then I was three over after five and my dreams were being broken. They would eventually be shattered.

That defeat in the Smurfit European Open was a tough one to take and not just because my good friend came through to snatch the title out of my grasp. I'd shot 60 and 66 in two of the three previous rounds, but couldn't buy a putt on the last day and shot a 75. Lee played fantastic golf and overhauled me and I was a disconsolate figure afterwards.

The thing that hurt the most was the feeling that I'd let the home fans down because nobody from Ireland had won on home soil since John O'Leary in 1982 at the Irish Open. Leaving the clubhouse that night, I ran into Dermot Desmond, the Irish businessman and financier, who I'd known for some time. He gave me a pat on the back and said, 'Battle on. What doesn't kill you makes you stronger.' Sound advice, but it definitely hurt at the time.

It took me a while to bounce back, because I'd gone through the full gamut of emotions that week – from massive highs to desperate lows. It was a defeat which definitely left its mental scars.

I went into the last event of the 2000 season, the WGC-American Express Championship at Valderrama, leading the money list and in a position to add the Order of Merit title to my CV. This time losing out to Lee again would not hurt a tenth as much.

Lee played great that week while I was so-so. That season, I'd won a huge cheque at the **WGC-Andersen Consulting Match Play** in Carlsbad, California, and the **English Open**, while Lee had collected five trophies and finished second and third twice each, with another five top-tens. By my calculation, he deserved to win the Order of Merit and I didn't.

I would still love to have a number one on the money list, but that comes through playing consistently well, and consistency has never been my thing.

My demise at the K Club may not have been forgotten, but the pain was significantly eased when I won the **European Open** there in 2001, and so became that golfer from Ireland to win on home soil.

Although stroke-play tournaments are over 72 holes, the key to this win centred on just one – the 17th, or rather the 71st. In the third round, I'd pulled my drive on this slight dog-leg and finished in the River Liffey. I then pushed my next shot right, on the way to making a seven. When I arrived on the same tee twenty-four hours later, I was leading by one over Padraig Harrington and a three or five wood off the tee would have been an easier and possibly wiser choice. But I went with the driver again and ripped it round the corner.

It was just one of those cases where I said to myself, 'If I'm going to win I'm going to win properly.' This philosophy has cost me on several occasions, but I wasn't going to shirk from hitting the driver when I thought it was the club to hit just because I had messed it up the day before. This time there were cheers rather than tears as I won by three shots from Thomas Bjørn, Padraig and Ian Woosnam.

My command of the Compass Group **English Open** continued at the Forest of Arden in 2002, where Søren Hansen, Raphaël Jacquelin and Phillip Price were my nearest challengers. My three-shot win meant I was the first player in its twenty-three-year history to win it three times.

It would be nearly six years before I won again on the European Tour, although in the intervening years I would twice come away with the spoils in the **Visa Taiheiyo Masters** in Japan, to add to my **Chunichi Crowns** success there in 2001 – a year when I also won the **Dimension Data Pro-Am** tournament in South Africa.

The Japanese love their golf and it was another road trip Lee and I used to go on regularly. We always enjoyed it, not least because they have some of the best greens in the world and excellent courses.

My win in the 2005 Visa Taiheiyo was my fifteenth overall, but I wasn't particularly proud, as I couldn't help thinking that I had underachieved throughout my career. Others may disagree, but that's my opinion and it still stands today.

The **2008 BMW Asian Open** produced late drama and I almost threw it away, before hanging on for what was a very emotional win. Three putts on the 16th during the last round

– the second from two feet – gave Dutchman Robert-Jan Derksen a chance, and another bogey at the 17th meant we went into the final hole joint leaders.

I had to gather my thoughts and dig deep and was thankful to see my final drive come to rest in the middle of the fairway, while Robert was long but off the short grass. My eight-iron approach was a little conservative and finished 40 feet left of the flag. I was playing safe because Robert had flown the green and didn't have much of a pitch. Unbelievably, he pitched up almost dead. It didn't seem possible he could get it to three feet from where he was, but he did. It was nothing less than a brilliant shot.

So I stood over my putt, telling myself to give it a go. As soon as I hit it, I knew it was carrying too much pace and would finish at least five or six feet past. But it kept tracking towards the hole, hit the back of the cup, jumped up and dropped in. It was a very big moment for me because it was my first win since Heather had died. Carmel Treacy, one of the Tour's recorders, was very sympathetic as I shed a few tears – giving me a pat on the back, totally understanding the moment.

The next win was nearly as important, but in a different context. Ryder Cup captain Nick Faldo had said he wanted to pick guys for the 2008 Ryder Cup who were in form, so I knew I needed a good week at that year's **KLM Open**, the week before qualifying ended. It was better than good – I won by four shots from Paul McGinley.

Both boys were with me and housekeeper Alice and they had a great week, walking every hole, so it was very pleasing to play as I did. I was in really good form and I definitely thought I'd done enough to make the team, especially since I was under heavy pressure. I was very happy with how I played in those circumstances, but sadly it wasn't enough to warrant one of the captain's picks.

Apart from the wins, other memorable moments from my twenty years on Tour would have to include the two 60s – in the Monte Carlo Open at Mont Agel in 1992 and the European Open at the K Club in 1999. The odd thing was that in Monte Carlo, I couldn't hit a cow's backside with a banjo on the range – duffing it, blocking it and generally hitting it everywhere it shouldn't have been going. But I went out on the course and absolutely flagged it – which just shows what a daft game this can be sometimes.

The 2006 Irish Open at Carton House in County Kildare was notable for something unique in European Tour history. I went on to finish third in the tournament, but finished up winning Shot of the Month . . . for an 80-yard pitch shot from the rough, back on to the fairway.

I was leading the tournament at the time and had hit a terrible tee shot off the 11th into thigh-high rough when the hooter went because of bad weather and play was suspended until the following morning.

The night before, I'd had no shot, but when I got to my ball on the Monday, the leprechauns had been out and flattened all the grass around the ball, leaving a perfect lie.

If I'd hit the shot the night before it would have had to be just a chip out on to the fairway and go from there. As soon as I saw what had happened overnight I called in the referee. After a long deliberation, I was told that no one had seen anybody do anything around my ball, so as far as they were concerned it was the rub of the green and I was entitled to play what I wanted. I said I wasn't comfortable with that, but they insisted it was within the rules, so I should carry on.

I didn't like it and I couldn't do it. From the minute I'd seen where the ball was and all the grass flattened around it I knew I had no option but to just chip it back into play. Now I was being told I could play for the green. The ruling may have been right, but I thought it was wrong.

Instead of going for the green, I hit the shot I would have hit the night before. If I had gone for the green and then proceeded to win the tournament, I would never have forgiven myself. I knew Bobby Jones would not have gone for the green; nor would Jack Nicklaus or any of the greats. Never mind what anyone else thought, my conscience was clear.

I've been known to call penalties on myself before. If there has been any shadow of a doubt then I'll call it against myself. Always have, always will. But if I think I've done the right thing and someone else tells me I haven't, then I'll get annoyed, particularly if I think someone is questioning my honesty on the golf course – simply because I have never in my career knowingly broken the rules. I couldn't anyway, my conscience wouldn't let me do it. You either win fairly and squarely or not at all. Your result should be a true reflection of how you've played, not how you've abused and broken the rules. Unfortunately, a few people on the Tour don't share the same opinion, and that's sad.

9

THE MAJORS

The Open Championship

My introduction to major championships came at the Open at **Royal Birkdale** in 1991. I remember it with a mixture of pride and acute embarrassment.

There was nothing to be proud of during an opening 79. I had to produce something special if I was to continue my involvement after the second round. Not only did I respond with a fighting 67, but I also hit a spectator . . . and it wasn't just any spectator, but probably the most famous wife in golf at the time and probably even now.

I pulled my tee shot on 16, hit somebody in the distance and walked down the fairway, not feeling too happy about it. I was absolutely mortified to discover that my ball had hit none other than Mrs Barbara Nicklaus. The Golden Bear's wife had disappeared by the time I got there, probably to find a tin helmet, and was thankfully none the worse for her encounter with an unidentified flying object. I didn't even get the chance to apologise.

Birkdale was the professional continuation of my amateur infatuation with links golf and I was delighted to have made all four rounds on such an impressive course. Obviously I've got an affiliation with links, growing up in Ireland. If I had a choice what sort of golf I'd play for the rest of my days, I'd definitely choose links every time. The courses can change every day and for me links golf is the truest form of the game. It's where the game was invented, after all. So to play all the links courses on the Open roster is a huge pleasure for me.

Birkdale is one of my favourites because it's very fair. Hoylake definitely deserves its place too, despite the funky internal out of bounds on the first, while Turnberry is many people's links of choice, and for good reasons. It's a fantastic venue – challenging, hard but fair, and for the most part you can see everything in front of you.

St Andrews is like a fine wine. Its beauty is not immediately identifiable and it takes years to appreciate it. I remember playing there for the first time and wondering what all the fuss was about. But the more you play it, the more you appreciate its quirky nature and understand why golf pilgrims from around the world flock to it every year. It is nothing short of fantastic. The closest I have got there was in 2000, seventh behind Tiger when he was winning majors for fun. I can't remember much about the week because everybody was in awe of what Tiger was doing. I doubt that anybody will ever achieve what he did there – not hitting one bunker all week was unbelievable.

Although I'd finished tied eleventh at Lytham in 1996, it was the following year at **Troon** where my first introduction to major championship contention arrived. The Ayrshire diamond is another delightful links course, possibly best known for its Postage Stamp hole – a much-admired tiny par three of just 123 yards. Underestimate it at your peril. My birdie there on Saturday moved me four clear and I was really enjoying myself, having a great time and looking forward to the final round.

Today, whenever long-standing spectators and supporters of the game think about Troon in 1997, they invariably associate it with the day I had a shank on the second tee. This is my opportunity to set the record straight once and for all. Playing with Jesper Parnevik in the final group, I parred the first hole and then took a four iron from the second tee. It's not a particularly challenging hole, about 400 yards, as long as you hit left off the tee. I hit right – all of 220 yards on to the beach. It was universally described as a shank that would cost me two shots and ultimately the main prize.

All I will say is that if that was a shank, I'd like to hit more of them, because that's a long, long way for a shank. But anyway, it did rattle me, and although I hung in there for the rest of the round, nothing happened for either me or Jesper, and Justin Leonard came through to claim the title. A birdie on the last gave me a share of second.

Carnoustie is arguably the toughest on the roster and has a brutal finish. Locals say the only thing you can predict on their course is its unpredictability, and that was certainly the case in 1999. Paul Lawrie started the last round ten shots behind and won. Jean Van de Velde started the last hole three shots ahead and lost. It's easy to understand what the locals mean, with 16 being a tougher-than-tough par three, 17 a treacherous par four and out of bounds to the left and water in front of the final hole.

Royal Lytham & St Annes is the oddest of the Open courses, but only because it's the furthest from the sea and starts with a par three. It also has a railway line running alongside the first few holes, making it quite a small plot of land. But in every other way it deserves total respect because it's a very fair golf course, demanding that you shape your shots both ways. Good ball-strikers love Lytham.

Another opportunity to win came there in 2001, when David Duval eventually claimed the big prize. From tee to green I played as well as I ever had up to that stage, but it was not meant to be. The putter was stone-cold all week, but I remember being one behind with a couple to play and my caddie, Billy Foster, wanted me to hit three wood off the 17th. I fancied the driver more and went with it.

There was a bunker at 310 yards into the wind, which I was convinced was out of reach. I hit a lovely, little low punch with the driver, but got a wicked shooting bounce and the ball trickled into the trap. The sands of time ran out for me too because I could only chop the ball out. I went for the flag with the third, found another bunker and took another three to get down. The double bogey would lead to me finishing third.

Muirfield, the home of the Honourable Company of Edinburgh Golfers, is another wonderful test, but in 2002 it would be remembered for the horrible weather which drenched and blew away just about everybody apart from South Africa's finest, Ernie Els.

I was on the first tee on the Saturday when the weather came in and the course was nigh on unplayable, even for someone who grew up playing an awful lot of links. It was nothing short of brutal, and even Tiger couldn't break 80.

There was nothing much to write home about on my first two visits to the Open at **Royal St George's**. I was not immediately impressed when I turned up in Greg Norman's year of 1993. I wasn't sure what was going on at all. I would hit off the tee, think I had a good line, but find my ball in the rough – the ball having bounced there because of the severe slopes on the fairways. And when the Open returned in 2003, who could not feel disappointment for Thomas Bjørn when he took three to get out of a bunker at the side of 16 and lost out to rookie winner Ben Curtis.

The Open had not been to **Hoylake** for thirty-nine years when it was held there in 2006, when Tiger gave another masterclass – this time using the driver just once all week on a course where the ball would run for ever. I remember it not so much for missing the cut, but for it being the day I declared I would not be playing golf for the foreseeable future.

The following year, I would play only two rounds at **Carnoustie**, but I watched every shot of the weekend as Padraig Harrington won the first of his back-to-back Opens. Padraig played so nicely, but Irish hearts were in mouths as he looked to be making too many mistakes on the last hole, only to get up and down for double bogey. It was only just enough to get into a play-off, because Spain's Sergio García lipped out for the win and then lost in the subsequent four-hole shoot-out.

Needing to pre-qualify in 2008 and failing over two rounds at

Sunningdale, when I played really poorly, was hard to take, given how much the Open means to me. I did make all four rounds the following year at Turnberry, but with all due respect to the eventual champion Stewart Cink and the unbelievable runner-up Tom Watson, it would have been great to have watched Lee Westwood win. If not Lee, then what a story it would have been had Tom, at 59, become the oldest champion, and by many years. The five-time former champion hit a great shot into 18, which took a really hard bounce and went through the back. At least 99 per cent of those watching were willing him to get up and down, which Tom sadly failed to do . . . and the same for Lee when his approach out of a bunker came up on the front of the green. He thought he had to hole the putt, went long and missed the one back that would have put him in the play-off. His day will come.

When we returned to **St Andrews** in 2010, Chubby was still looking for his first major as a manager, but four days after the first shot was hit, South African Louis Oosthuizen would put right that particular omission. Louis is a fantastic ball-striker, a great young kid, and he showed the world what he was made of that week, winning by a street, with Lee a distant second and not really having been in contention – that was how well the winner played.

The majors I haven't won . . . yet

Memorable personal moments in my visits to the other three majors – the Masters, the US Open, the US PGA – are not particularly vivid, which probably has something to do with the fact that

I have only had three top-ten finishes in thirty-five starts and have missed the weekend action on sixteen occasions.

I've fared best at the **Masters**, and the top-ten I had there was on my first visit in 1998. I thought Augusta was brilliant as soon as I saw it and my opinion has never changed; it is still a very special place to go and play. What has changed is the setting-up of the course. In my first year, there was no rough and then the following year there was, and it's been there ever since.

My results say I preferred it with no rough, because when the leaders teed off on that Sunday I was already five under for the round through 11 and really charging up the board. Then I committed a schoolboy error. I let my concentration slip as my playing partner hit into the water and took a while to get his angles right before eventually hitting on to the green.

By this time I'd lost my focus, hit my first putt five feet past, missed the one coming back, dropped a shot and totally lost momentum. I parred all the way in and eventually finished eighth. I've made six of ten cuts in my following visits and played averagely, nothing great.

The **US Open** has never been my cup of tea, as my record shows – one tenth and nothing else inside the top twenty in eleven other visits. I don't know why I have not done better. After all, I am a reasonable driver of the ball, which is paramount at US Open set-ups. It's probably understandable that my best finish – tenth in 1999 – came at Pinehurst, which has more of a links feel to it than any other course on the US Open roster.

The **US PGA** is a complete mystery to me. They don't set up the courses as tough as their Open venues, but my record is far worse – nine missed cuts out of thirteen visits is a record I don't need reminding of too often. My PGA top-ten, a ninth, came at Valhalla in 2000, but the other results are eminently forgettable. I'm at a loss to understand why my record in the season's final major is so poor, but I've got time to rectify it.

The World Golf Championships

Now, WGC events are another matter altogether. My first win, and the one that really got me noticed in America, came in 2000 when I most memorably beat Tiger in the final of the **WGC-Andersen Consulting Match Play** in California.

It was another case of me turning up believing that Chubby had more chance of winning it than me. In fact, that's not as daft as it sounds, because I'd missed the cut at Riviera the previous week and we'd arrived at La Costa early. We went out and played on the other course there and, as if my confidence wasn't low enough already, Chubby beat me 6&5. Yes – 6&5. He was always one for negotiating more shots than he deserved and got the hump if he didn't get them, but he beat me fair and square on this occasion.

It seemed to be pointless teeing up the following Wednesday. 'If I can't beat Chubby,' I thought to myself, 'then what chance do I have against the world's best? I'd be better off going home.' But I stayed, and as soon as the gun went off I started hitting the target. First I beat Paul Azinger 2&1, then Mark O'Meara 5&4, and then I had to face my practice partner Thomas Bjørn.

My match-play record compares to many, particularly when I am not running around like a headless chicken. This was one of those occasions. For some reason, I was relaxed and comfortable all week – having a quiet dinner with a glass or two of wine and a cigar with Chubby and Louis Martin. When I'm in that kind of mood, I always play well.

I had been pretty consistent against Paul and Mark but more wayward against Thomas, although still hitting plenty of greens and making a few putts. And I was telling myself that if I could get this far, there was no reason not to go all the way. Five days after wanting to get out of there, I had a chance to head home with the pot and a million dollars.

My next opponent was Hal Sutton, who had beaten me in the Brookline singles at the Ryder Cup. For four holes it looked as if I'd walked into the same buzz saw. I had plenty of respect for Hal before we started, but it would grow over the first four holes, and I walked on to the fifth tee three down and pleading with him, 'Take it easy on me.'

Hal boomed another straight down the middle. My tee shot was heading into the right rough, if not further into no-man's-land, when something happened that would change the course of the match completely. I was expecting to hit my next shot from a tough position, but instead it was from the tee again. It turns out I'd hit an overhead power cable and I was allowed to reload without penalty. I promptly blasted one past Hal, hit a four-iron approach straight to the flag, birdied the hole and he couldn't match it. From thinking I would be four down, it was back to two. I never looked back. Sometimes it just clicks, and that day was one of those occasions.

It went just as well against another friend, David Duval, in the semi-final. I had one of those rounds when the ball never left the centre of the club. We shook hands and David said, 'Good luck tomorrow with the thirty-six holes.' I thought I was hearing things, so I checked with him. 'It's not thirty-six, is it?'

I wasn't at my most athletic at that stage, in fact I was more like a boiled egg on stilts, but thirty-six holes would have to be done. From starting the week a no-hoper, I was heading for a final showdown with Tiger. What a funny old game.

On the morning of the final, I had breakfast with Tiger, our caddies, Steve Williams and Billy Foster, Chubby and Butch Harmon. Butch was the only guy at the table who couldn't lose, because he coached both of us. I'd got to know Tiger a lot more through Butch and we'd always got on well. So well that all week long I'd been winding him up about the fact that I was 1–0 up over him at match play, because Lee and I had beaten him and David Duval at the 1999 Ryder Cup on the one occasion we'd played.

I don't know what made me think of it while we were chewing the bacon fat over breakfast, but I remembered Tiger once having chipped in at Muirfield Village and running round the green doing very animated fist pumps.

'Hey Tiger,' I said. 'If you chip in today and start one of those ******* exaggerated celebrations running round the green and fist-pumping, then I'll give you a slap across the face.'

To which Tiger replied something along the lines of 'Go away, you overweight sod; you couldn't catch me anyway.'

If my message to Tiger was said with a smile on my face, there was an element of truth, because I have always been very keen on etiquette. The game means a great deal to me and I firmly believe it should always be played in the right manner. It's a matter of showing respect for your opponent, something I have tried to adhere to from day one.

I may have put a fist-clenched arm out occasionally, but only if it was to recognise something which really did mean something. On the Sunday when you've won a tournament, that's fine. I've seen guys fist-pumping after holing a three-footer on the third hole. What a load of nonsense. It just sits uncomfortably with me.

Previous generations of players didn't do it and I tell my boys not to do it now. That's not to say the guys that do it are wrong, but I just don't see the game that way. At the end of the day, if you don't respect the game, its etiquette and the way it should be played, then you shouldn't be doing it. My motto is: Do it properly or not at all.

I was sure that Tiger knew exactly where I was coming from when talking about histrionics. Now I had to hope he didn't know where I was coming from on the course.

Fortunately, I continued in the same vein as I had the previous rounds. I hit a lot of little knock-down shots, controlled the spin and managed to sink enough putts to give me confidence that it might just be my day, as long as Tiger wasn't at his best. He wasn't.

There wasn't a great deal of time between the end of the first round and the start of the second, but Tiger wasn't going to waste any of it. He headed straight for the range, obviously not satisfied at being all square after eighteen. My abiding memory was of him rushing down to practise.

I took one look at the steep hill going down to the practice area, realised I would have to walk back up it if I went down and immediately decided that I'd done enough walking. I sat down on a concrete wall at the top of the hill, lit a cigar and talked to Heather on the phone. I couldn't be bothered to practise.

Happily, I was able to pick up where we'd left off when we restarted. Tiger had an off day, I had a good day and we eventually shook hands with the match ending 4&3 in my favour.

If Tiger had played anywhere near his best – he won the US Open that year by fifteen shots, don't forget – then neither I nor anybody else could have touched him. I was lucky that he had an off day. I don't want that to come across as patronising, but he just wasn't quite at the races and I was.

By the time I'd done the presentation ceremony and the media, Tiger was long gone, but he'd left a note on my locker. 'Congratulations, be proud.' There was a PS, however, with a ruder comment about my physique. I have the note framed at home.

I think Tiger respected me a bit more than just as a friend after that match. I'd not shied away from anything and in those days everybody was falling backwards for him. It was indeed a proud moment to realise I had beaten the best in the world at the time and arguably of all time.

To win something as big as the WGC Match Play had always been a possibility. I'd had the potential for the past few years but never finished the job off, letting quite a few opportunities to win tournaments slip through my fingers. But that day I'd been very solid, hit fairways and greens and been 11 under for the thirty-three holes played. To have played like that under the circumstances against Tiger was certainly very gratifying. I was 31 at the time and the win would prove a great stepping stone for me.

It took me three years to prove I wasn't 'one and done' with WGC events, however. Winning the 2003 **WGC-NEC Invitational** at Firestone in Akron, Ohio, was a massive milestone for me because it meant I was the first player after Tiger to win more than one WGC event . . . and I would hold that honour for quite some time.

When I arrived I wasn't entirely happy with my game – there wasn't a lot new in that – but perseverance with a training aid paid a big dividend. I'd been using an arm bracelet for the past month and I had a feeling it was helping my timing and generally sharpening my swing. Butch Harmon had brought it over for me at the Open at Royal St George's earlier that summer and its main purpose was to stop my right arm collapsing at the top of the swing, which in turn made my swing shorter and wider. It would do the trick.

It's always a pleasure to go to Akron because not only is Firestone one of America's finest courses, but in Ken Stewart's

Grille it also has one of the country's best restaurants. I enjoyed both all week. We have our favourite eating places at every Tour stop, through years of experience. Some stay on the list and others fall off, but in Ken Stewart's the quality of food and service has never varied over two decades. I have no hesitation in saying that Firestone is one of the best courses we play anywhere in the world. It's not easy by any means, but it is extremely fair and that's all we ask.

It was also a relief to be there after the rigours of the previous week at the US PGA Championship at Oak Hill in Rochester, New York State. The Firestone rough was penal in places, but not the jungle it had been around the greens at Oak Hill. At least missing the cut had given me more time to practise at Firestone and get used to the firm and fast conditions I enjoy.

That season, I had been quietly proud of my patience, which was a quality I had not been able to display enough in the past. When I play well I can play very well, but it just hasn't happened as much as I would have liked. It isn't through lack of work, just that sometimes it doesn't happen. Previously, I had tended to get very annoyed with myself, but throughout 2003 my attitude had been very good indeed. I was letting things happen, for a change, and now it looked as if there might be a return at last.

On the final day I was looking for a fast start to match the conditions, and they don't come much faster than an eagle at the second, but there were no thoughts of winning at that stage because Firestone can jump up and grab you anywhere along the route. I didn't get ahead of myself at any point and the first look I had at a leader board was after 13. Not only was Tiger chasing me, but Jonathan Kaye was in the second to last group and every time I made a birdie, so did he. It made for a very exciting day. It ended as a very good one.

Hurdle after hurdle was safely negotiated and I was able to hold on, although I approached the last green not quite knowing how many I had to win, but I knew I had enough. It was a feeling that would return eight years later with an even greater prize awaiting.

After the majors and possibly the Players Championship at Sawgrass, I think most players would place WGC events next on their list of must-wins. So to have two of them was very pleasing. I wasn't sure which had given me greater pleasure. The Match Play had been exactly that – head to head against one guy at a time – whereas this was not just Tiger, but the rest of the world's best, all waiting for me to make enough mistakes for them to sneak through. Thing was, I did what I had to and it was enough.

10

THE RYDER CUP

Playing in the Ryder Cup was always high up on my must-do list. There is nothing to compare with it in a golfing representative sense. I'd played a lot of team golf as an amateur and I really enjoyed the competition and camaraderie, so I was keen to test myself in this ultimate golfing arena. Man against man, team against team: since continental Europe was added to the initial Great Britain and Ireland representation, Sam Ryder's pot of gold has become the most coveted prize.

1997, Valderrama:
Europe 14½ – 13½ United States

My first opportunity to play came in 1997, although the bookmakers did not give much for my chances or those of my good friend and ISM stablemate Lee Westwood. We were quite highly priced and we both took the opportunity to pit our skills against those of the oddsmakers.

It also challenged Chubby's management skills, and he would ultimately emerge victorious. Chubby had noticed that in previous qualification processes those players who were in with a shout of making the team, particularly rookies, often suffered a loss of form because they were trying too hard and thinking about it too much. So, at the start of the build-up, he urged Lee and me not to think about the Ryder Cup, but to let it be a by-product of our goal for the season, which was to make the world's top fifty. He reasoned that if we achieved that, we were almost certain to make the team.

Consequently, we didn't treat the Ryder Cup as the be-all and end-all, but something that we might play in if we progressed and improved as players. Sure enough, we both made it, and it wasn't even a close thing. I finished second at Wentworth to Ian Woosnam in the Volvo PGA and that was me in the team from a very early stage. Lee was also over the line long before the scheduled finish. I headed for Spain having qualified second overall.

Our captain Seve Ballesteros spoke to the prospective team members at the Lancome Trophy in Paris and he also had a few, brief words with me individually, but that was all the contact I had with the great Spaniard before Europe and America's finest gathered on the Costa del Sol (ironically we hardly saw the sun all week).

Having the five-time major champion as captain when the match was in Spain for the first time was a huge deal. He was wired all week – hyper doesn't really do his demeanour justice. As American team member Tom Lehman commented afterwards, 'Every time I stepped on a tee, it seemed like Seve vaporised alongside. He was everywhere.'

It soon became clear that my high qualification counted for nothing. I arrived in Valderrama full of hope, expectation and excitement, but that was quickly knocked out of me by captain Seve when the first-day pairings were announced. At the time, I was not experienced enough to deal with the decision to leave me out of both series of matches. I was disappointed, to say the least, and Chubby had to convince me that it wouldn't be right to disappear to my room or even leave the course altogether. This was a team event, he stressed.

I was able to vent some of my frustration on the captain himself. As luck would have it, my locker was right next to Seve's and at the first opportunity while we were changing, I made my feelings known to him. I have never been one to shy away from anything, so I wanted to get it off my chest.

My problem wasn't so much to do with not playing as the way I discovered that I wasn't. It was my opinion that the guys being left out should be told face to face. I actually discovered my lot through watching television and, to put it diplomatically, I took a little bit of exception to it. The media knew my fate before I did and that annoyed me. I told Seve what I thought. I didn't get much of a response, although to be honest I'm not sure what it was at all, because no sooner had I finished than he lapsed from English into Spanish, and my command of his language does not extend much beyond hola and rioja.

Of course, Seve did what he thought was best for the team and only now can I admit that he was perfectly correct. I would have liked to play and at the time I was very disappointed, but looking back on it now, and with the prospect of me being captain at some stage in the future, I can see just how difficult a job it is to balance everything. As a young guy, very keen to get out there, I couldn't see the full picture.

My first match was not until the Saturday, when I was paired with the team's talisman, Colin Montgomerie, to play against Davis Love III and Freddie Couples in the fourballs. I had no say in the matter whatsoever, but it was great to be paired with somebody like Monty. I was also delighted to be playing against people I was familiar with. Davis and Freddie are both fantastic guys who went on to become very good friends.

Anybody who is not nervous at the Ryder Cup is not human. When it was my turn to hit on the first tee, all I wanted to do was make contact, so I teed it a little higher than normal just to ensure some part of the club caught the ball. To my relief, and probably Monty's, I did not have a fresh-air, but I tugged the ball a tad and it finished behind a lone tree in the left rough.

As the senior member of the partnership, Monty came over to see everything was all right and to weigh up what I was considering. My options were either to go under and around the tree's branches or through a 'V' in the tree. That was a bit of a dodgy shot, but I thought I could do it.

I said to him, 'I'm going to try to hit it through that "V". What do you think?'

His reply brooked no debate. 'For heaven's sake, it's the Ryder Cup,' he said. 'Just punch it low somewhere up around the green and see what develops.' That's what I did.

The match was always in the balance and apart from stiffing it on the 14th, I can't remember too much about what happened until we arrived on the 17th tee all square. There is trouble everywhere on this hole – off the tee, with your second shot and around and on the green. Five is not a bad score on this Seve creation, and that was what one of us would have to get to avoid going behind.

I found the rough with my tee shot and had a dodgy lie, but with his own ball safely on the fairway (in those days he rarely missed them), Monty encouraged me to have a go for it. I actually hit a decent shot, but it didn't carry quite far enough and the ball rolled back into the water. The pressure was firmly on Monty, but after laying up, he played an absolutely wonderful pitch – it was a little soft lobber to about five feet. It was just sheer class and really impressed me, and it was fitting that he went on to hole the putt for a hole-winning birdie.

The 18th at Valderrama is another very tough hole, particularly off the tee, and it does not offer up many birdies. We were determined to give ourselves two chances to make par at worst. Monty pulled his tee shot into the left rough and I hit a really good one down the middle. Freddie drove right and had no approach, while Davis was a little further down the fairway than me.

I was in a good place both physically with my ball and mentally in my head, but Seve came over just as I was preparing to play. He was almost in the bag, pulling out the clubs to see what we were going to hit, when my caddie Billy said, 'Seve, get the **** out of the way. Go away.'

While I might have been thinking it, Billy was actually saying it, which wasn't too surprising, because the pair had been very good friends and fairway colleagues for a long time. But I doubt that any other player or caddie would have felt confident enough to speak to him like that.

Seve did as asked and I hit a lovely shot straight down the flag, 15 feet short of the hole. Under those circumstances it was a really good effort and I was delighted that I would have a chance of getting the half that would secure the full point.

Monty had hit a good shot out of the rough to about 30 feet right of the pin. They went first and missed, so we had two putts from either of us to win. I had 15 feet up the hill and a little bit right to left and I wanted to hit the putt, but Monty called seniority, lagged his 30-footer down alongside the hole and they conceded the match. My ball was not needed, but I'd certainly take those two shots any time I play that hole.

I did not participate again until the Sunday singles, when I would take on Phil Mickelson, one of America's finest.

There were outside forces driving me to do as much as I possibly could to win. Chubby, as he frequently does, had one of his wonderful bonus schemes going for me, which meant that I would collect if I won every game I played at the Ryder Cup, as long as I played at least two. So here I was with a 100 per cent record after one match, knowing that, if I completed a double against Phil, I would drive away from Valderrama in a Ferrari F40, courtesy of my then clubmakers, MacGregor.

I actually wasn't thinking about that when we went out to play – well, not much. It was somewhere in the back of my mind, I suppose. But Phil, as Phil can so often do, chipped in a couple of times, played very nicely and beat me on the 17th. MacGregor were spared their bonus, although I don't think they would have minded handing over the keys, and not just for the coverage they would have received.

All in all, it was a fantastic experience to be part of a success-ful team. Winning is everything in the Ryder Cup and I think it was very fitting, although it was a magnificent team effort, that Monty was the man who sealed the success that Seve demanded. Seve's passion for the game shone through; he really was not going to lose that week. Whatever it took, Seve was going to find it, give it, do it. He did. The relief was very evident to see, not only the joy of winning, but the release. He never wanted to lose anywhere, but under no circumstances did he want to go down in Spain.

The celebrations were long and typical, but it marked the end of an old ritual – the post-match joint dinner with our opponents. They stopped it afterwards, determining that the vanquished should not be subjected to seeing the unbridled joy of their oppo-nents as well as listening to endless speeches. Dinners and speeches have their places, but after the Ryder Cup these days is not one of them.

1999, Brookline:
United States 14½ – 13½ Europe

From the rain in Spain to the breezes of Boston in 1999, where America under Ben Crenshaw would host a European team led by Mark 'Jesse' James.

Despite having some of the most ironic television shows to be found anywhere on the planet, Americans can have a problem coping with English sarcasm and Jesse is capable of ladling it out in copious quantities. I get his dry sense of humour but, more often than not, it gets halfway across the Atlantic and then the jet stream brings it straight back home. Some of his funniest lines during the week at Brookline seemed to fly higher over their heads than the Concorde on which we had arrived.

Throughout the week, the team never missed a Jesse press conference and we would be in stitches as his deadpan delivery seemed to amuse some but confuse others. Asked what his most difficult decision in one session had been, he replied, 'Whether to have the burger or chicken sandwich for lunch.' The irony of that particular retort was that he was being absolutely truthful, but try telling that to the Americans.

To me, Jesse was Captain Fantastic – the way he conducted himself, ran the team and represented our continent. It was a great pity that it didn't work out for him, but unfortunately that would be his destiny after a great week.

*   *   *

Memories of my first morning foursomes match with Lee Westwood against Hal Sutton and Jeff Maggert are few and far between – not surprising since we lost 3&2. But I can remember just about every shot in the afternoon fourballs, when we paired up again to face the number one and number two in the world at the time, Tiger Woods and David Duval. It was just a fantastic opportunity to be pitted against golf's top two. Despite our morning setback, we were both playing fairly nicely at the time and relished the prospect of a great match.

Lee made a few birdies and I weighed in here and there with some of my own, but we knew they'd give as good as they got, and by the time we stood on the 17th tee we were exactly as we started – with everything to play for and just two holes to claim very notable scalps.

Lee had equalled the fours of Tiger and David and after a decent tee shot and a better wedge, I had 12 feet left for what would be a winning birdie to ensure that we could not lose the match. As soon as the putter made contact with the ball, I knew where it was going and I wasn't disappointed when it disappeared bang in the centre of the hole.

One up with one to go and two chances to equal the best they could do for an outright win that we knew would give a huge boost to the team in the final match of the afternoon.

My ball drifted right off the 18th tee, but Lee was in prime position in the fairway on what isn't really a birdie hole, so we weren't in bad shape. Then neither Tiger nor David could get close, but I was off the right edge of the green and Lee came up short and was in some rough. At that stage of his career, Lee wasn't the short-game wizard he is these days. It was his turn to go first and the light was fading, so I think we both had our fingers crossed, because I wasn't certain of getting up and down either.

Anyway, Lee hit a career recovery and the ball snuggled up cosily to the hole for what would be a match-deciding half. I'm not really into man hugs, but we gave each other the biggest we had ever had. In match-play fourballs, somebody tends to come in more than their partner, but we'd been perfect foils for one another and our reward was to have taken down the top two players in the world. It was an unbelievable feeling.

Any lead at the end of the first day would have been more than acceptable, but our win meant that over supper that night we would be staring at a four-point supremacy – unprecedented for a European team on American soil.

I can usually remember something about winning matches, but just to show that my memory can betray me sometimes, on Saturday Lee and I defeated Mark O'Meara and Jim Furyk in the morning foursomes 3&2 and I do not remember one shot that either side hit.

There was plenty to recall from the afternoon fourball encounter against Phil Mickelson and Tom Lehman – a match which had plenty of edge and went all the way to the wire. At the time, I didn't know either of the Americans as well as I do now, and there was a bit of niggle which centred on them thinking that we were slow-playing them, practice-putting for too long after the holes had been finished. Nothing could have been further from the truth, but they obviously felt we were.

They were both playing great, while we were struggling to get anything going, but we had a good chance to get back into the game when I left myself a short uphill birdie putt on the par-five 10th. It was looking good for us, because Tom was the best placed of their side and he had a 30-footer across the green with a massive amount of swing on it. Unbelievably, he holed it and immediately set off on a celebration around the green – before I had taken my putt.

Now, you can celebrate any way you want if you have won the hole and your opponents don't have anything to finish off, but I still had my four-footer, which was now for a half rather than a win, and he should have waited.

I did hole my putt, but I gave Tom the biggest stare I have ever given anybody on a course after it dropped in.

The niggle between the two sides did not end there. A few holes later, we'd hit a couple of practice putts after a hole was finished and we got to the next tee and Tom teed off.

Nobody moved and then Lee turned to Phil and said, 'Are you not going to hit?'

Phil replied, 'I already have.'

Phil had taken his shot before we were anywhere near the tee, and although he had not broken any rules, etiquette should have dictated that he wait until we had got there. He was within his rights, but that was not the proper etiquette in my book.

I've grown close to both players since then and appreciate they were just doing what they felt they had to. No matter what had happened, they were deserving winners and we shook hands on the 17th green.

It was still an enthusiastic team room that Saturday night because we knew we were going into the final series of singles with a bigger lead than any previous visiting team in America in the history of the entire competition. We were 4 points ahead, needing another 4½ from the 12 available on that fateful Sunday.

On the day, everybody was looking forward to it, knowing we'd built up such a good lead, and our hope was to improve it as soon as possible. Jesse sent Lee and me out one and two, and I'm sure he was thinking that we'd get at least one point from the two matches to consolidate and give us impetus. It didn't go according to plan, as we lost to Tom and Hal respectively. And behind us were three players who were playing their first matches of the week – Jarmo Sandelin, Jean Van de Velde and Andrew Coltart, who had all sat out the first two days of fourball and foursomes matches.

All of a sudden, from a commanding position we were on the back foot and America were coming at us with very heavy artillery. By the time Padraig Harrington secured Europe's first point of the afternoon, from the seventh match, America were ahead and not about to surrender their lead.

Much of what was said and written afterwards centred on events on the 17th green when Justin Leonard holed a monster putt and many Americans invaded the green and ran across José María Olazábal's line in premature victory celebration – again before the Spaniard had taken his putt. It goes back to what I was saying earlier, that you can celebrate as much as you like afterwards, but you should have respect for your opponent if he still has to go.

The Americans came in for a lot of criticism, but what was lost in the condemnation of their actions was just how well our hosts played that day. To employ one of their overused words, they were awesome. Their play was sensational and that should have been recognised.

We lost 14½–13½ and Jesse came in for a lot of flak. It is my contention that he did nothing wrong whatsoever throughout the entire week. Much of the criticism was about his decision not to play three players, all rookies, before the final day. But ask anybody who knows anything about it what scenario they would embrace going into the final day and 99 per cent, at the very least, will take a four-point lead.

Jesse thought – as did everybody else – that a Westwood-Clarke one-two, with the way we were playing, would produce at least a point. But it didn't and nothing came from the three rookies behind us – not that anybody blamed them at all. Our hosts gained an early impetus, and an American team with impetus is a dangerous animal indeed.

What's more, Jesse was not a one-man captain; he always consulted the entire team about everything, including the line-up for the Sunday singles. So we were all happy and comfortable with it, but it just didn't transpire. The same went for the team make-up before the singles. It was a hard decision to leave three players out for two days, but the way we were playing and the way the points were stacking up made it tricky. We had the biggest points lead ever in America, so how could Jesse be faulted for that? We were there to win as a team not just as individuals.

The team aspect and spirit of the Ryder Cup was personified by Payne Stewart, who conceded his match to Colin Montgomerie. The overall result had been determined, so he gave Monty the point, much as Seve instructed Monty, in a winning position, to give Scott Hoch a half in the deciding match at Valderrama when all we needed was a half. I had no problem with that. I know the bookies and a few others don't like it, but I'm not one of them.

That is one of the great things about the Ryder Cup. Commentators and pundits go on about highest points scorers and personal records, but to me that's a load of nonsense. It's wonderful to have a great winning record, but the overall team record is what matters. The guy who makes one point or half a point is as important as the guy who makes four or five points.

Losing at Brookline was a huge blow and we were all very down that evening. We had let a wonderful position go and I felt really bad for Jesse and the criticism he received from the media. We played very well for two days and they played brilliantly on the last. Jesse would have been a master tactician had we won, but instead he got hammered – unfairly in my opinion, because I thought he did a fantastic job.

2002, The Belfry:
Europe 15½ – 12½ United States

It would be three years not two before the next match because of the tragedy of 9/11 in 2001. We were about to play in the American Express in St Louis when the twin towers came down in New York and the world was rightly put on hold. The Ryder Cup, due to start at the Belfry a couple of weeks later, was put back twelve months and that's why it is now played in even-numbered years.

Sam Torrance had succeeded his good friend Mark James as Ryder Cup captain and was just as popular among the team members. Sam being Sam, everything was meticulous in preparation and he was very hands-on. He spoke to us all regularly in the build-up. Obviously, he knew his team from the year before anyway, but he took the time and effort to speak to us in depth and at length about everything. I have a very special place in my affections for Sam and not just because I'd worked with his dad. It had been him who had suggested I'd be better off turning professional all those years ago rather than staying amateur.

Though the Westwood-Clarke axis was split up on the first day, our collective success in the fourball format would continue with new partners on a fine morning for Europe. I was first out with Thomas Bjørn against Tiger Woods and Paul Azinger and there was an unbelievable electricity around the first tee – the extra year's wait adding to the excitement and anticipation. There were exposed nerves everywhere. Zinger had an iron out and then switched to a wood, while I think both Thomas and I were just hoping to make contact.

I pushed my tee shot a hair into the bunker on the right, but a fine recovery to 10 feet set up a birdie opportunity, which I converted. I did the same from 12 feet on the second and added a third on the next. I knew it wasn't about me, because this was team golf, but I'd grown up watching Seve and Sam and Gordon Brand Jnr playing this course and wondering how they were able to play so well under extreme pressure. Now I'd gone birdie, birdie, birdie over the first three holes of what was an unbelievable match. It culminated in Thomas holing a 25-footer on the final green to win the point. It was a great way to start the competition and our success was quickly followed by points from Lee alongside Sergio and Monty with Bernhard Langer.

The Bjørn–Clarke partnership was not as successful in the afternoon foursomes, however. We were probably a bit drained from our morning effort and we went down to Hal Sutton and Scott Verplank. But the important thing was that the team led after the first day by one point.

That lead was intact after the morning foursomes on the second day, although the Bjørn–Clarke pairing was again beaten, this time quite comfortably by Tiger and Davis Love. So Sam rang the changes in the afternoon and I went out with Paul McGinley to face Scott Hoch and Jim Furyk in the fourballs.

We had a very interesting tight game, reaching the last tee all square. I drove into the bunker on the right, while Paul was ahead of me and on the fairway. Because mine was a tricky recovery, Paul opted to hit first and produced a quite stunning shot to the top, and correct, level of the three-tier green. It was the right decision, because my ball didn't come out of the bunker as hoped and found the water, so it was over to Paul. He did not falter and secured the half, which meant that the sides were locked 8–8 after the first two days.

I was fully aware of the fact I hadn't won a Sunday singles match up to that point and if I was to break that duck it would not be at all easy – pitted against a good friend in David Duval. I got off to a decent start. He was a bit sluggish but fought back, and we were all square on the 17th tee. We traded birdies on the 17th after I'd holed from 25 feet, so it was still all to play for standing on the last tee.

David was short of the water in two on the par four after driving into a bunker, and I was in the right rough by the green. His third shot finished 12 feet short of the hole, while I pulled out a fantastic chip, which finished one foot away. I don't think I would have missed it, but David generously conceded the putt before putting a pure stroke on his ball and rolling it straight in for the half.

It can be awkward playing against a mate. The killer instinct is always there, because of course you want to win, but I'm certainly never that bothered if my opponent, particularly when it's a friend, hits a great shot like that.

We were all aware that the singles had been mainly dominated by the Americans in recent encounters, but we would not be denied, and it finally fell to Paul McGinley to hole the putt that put Sam Ryder's pot in Sam Torrance's hands.

I remember following Paul for those last few holes and the pressure was immense. He was left with a tricky up-and-down for a match-deciding half, but he finished it off by holing an eight-footer with a left-to-right break . . . straight in the middle, to the joy of millions and the sorrow of millions of others.

To this day, we still see clips of Paul holing the putt that ensured European victory and then a lady in blue-and-white checked trousers running across the green to congratulate him. It was my wife Heather.

2004, Oakland Hills:
United States 9½ – 18½ Europe

Apart from the blip in Boston, Europe was becoming dominant in Ryder Cup matches, and trips across the Atlantic were by no means as intimidating as they had been for Europe's Great Britain and Ireland predecessors. So I arrived in Oakland Hills in Michigan full of hope and optimism . . . and with a new partner, my fellow cigar-smoker Miguel Angel Jiménez.

I had one reservation, but not in the least with the Spaniard, because I have liked, admired and drunk many a red with him over a number of years. My problem was with one of Bernhard Langer's vice-captains, the Swede Anders Forsbrand, with whom

I had crossed swords some years earlier. For whatever reason, Bernhard had chosen Forsbrand alongside Thomas Bjørn, whom I was delighted to see in the team room.

My grouse with Forsbrand dated back to when we were playing once and I'd crossed a water hazard close to a green but the ball rolled back into it. He didn't agree that the ball had crossed, so I had to play from the other side of the water, even though I was 100 per cent sure I would have been entitled to drop at the front, because that's where I was certain it last touched ground before going in the hazard. I wasn't happy, yet I had no option but to go back. It's funny sometimes how these things work out, but later in the round somebody spotted that Forsbrand had taken a drop and played the ball from where he shouldn't have. I'd no idea he'd contravened the rules because I wasn't watching, but he went ahead and played his ball . . . only to be disqualified later.

Vice-captain selections are always quite a difficult thing to get right, but it helps if they've played Ryder Cup – and Anders had not. They have to know what players are going through, because it's not quite as straightforward and easy as it sounds. So that week my confidant was basically Thomas; I wanted nothing to do with Anders. It worked out fine, and I must say that captain Bernhard was not the only immense figure in the team room that week. Thomas was also a huge presence. He's a very astute man, knew all the players and had everybody's ear. He did a great job.

We knew we had a very strong team and I don't think it would have mattered much who played with whom, so I was more than happy to be out with Miguel. I couldn't help remember playing a practice round with him in 1999 at Brookline alongside José María Olazábal and Paul Lawrie. At that stage of his life, Miguel was prone to a little bit of hair tampering and I noticed that his curly locks were definitely edging towards a claret colour. It had been raining and, walking from the first green to the second tee, I grabbed Miguel's hat off his head and found on closer inspection that there was some reddish colour on the inside. Miguel did not see the funny side, but the other three of us certainly did. That's Miguel, bless him.

Anyway, at Oakland Hills we ham-and-egged perfectly against an in-form Chad Campbell, Tour Championship winner, and Davis Love. I started off fast and holed a few putts and we dove-tailed perfectly in the fourball format. If I wasn't there, he was, and vice versa. We had a round where everything went our way. They made a few mistakes and we made birdie when they did err, so we rode the momentum and never let them into the match. We shook hands on a 5&4 win.

The team had a great morning and we were three points up after the first session, a huge achievement and impetus-builder. That lead would be extended to five by the end of an afternoon which pitted myself and my old sparring partner Lee Westwood against another world number one and two pairing, this time Tiger Woods and Phil Mickelson.

How can I put it? Let's say we thought it was an interesting combination. American captain Hal Sutton had said at the pairings announcement that Tiger with Phil was something the world of golf wanted, he wanted and they wanted. That comment caused quite a bit of debate, particularly when they lost their morning fourball to Monty and Padraig Harrington.

I don't think that in those days Tiger and Phil actually saw eye to eye. There was an intense rivalry between them, which was healthy for the game, but they just weren't pals. Things have changed somewhat since, but they weren't close then and yet were paired together. As a result, there was always a chance of something going wrong with the team ethic and it not working out.

For my part, I was more than happy to go into those foursomes with Lee alongside, because apart from Seve and Chema (as José María is known), ours was the next most successful partnership in that format. On this day, we struggled a bit at first, however, and were several holes down early on. The dream pairing seemed to be living up to their billing.

I turned to Lee and said, 'Never fear. Keep patient and if we keep going, we'll get back into this game.'

I was trying to sound sensible, but I was actually convinced that was what we had to do. I was right, because we both started hitting good shots, made hole-winning birdies and arrived on the last tee all square.

Lee went first and absolutely ripped it up the fairway, while Phil, to the astonishment of all watching, made an out-of-the-blue terrible swing for him, which resulted in a big, high carve cut that ended against a fence and left Tiger no alternative but to take a drop. The best they could make was a six, while I had a six iron that came up a little short because the only nightmare for us would have been to go long. A chip and two putts and the point was ours – a bonus win, considering how we and they had started. It was the first day Tiger and Phil had played together as a pairing in the Ryder Cup . . . and they never have since.

I came across Tiger again the following morning, but this time he was alongside Chris Riley and I had Ian Poulter as my partner. It's always fun playing with Poults, because he's entertaining and has a great game; he's good value and top company. He wasn't as enthusiastic about me later, though, after I'd not played well and he had.

'******** to you,' he said. 'I've watched you play match after match, hole putt after putt, and you play with me and what happens? You can't hole a thing. Thank you very much.'

I can't remember what I replied, but it would have been something sympathetic . . . not.

I was back with Lee for the afternoon foursomes against Jay Haas and Chris DiMarco and it was business as usual. We know one another's game so well and always play to the other's strengths, so we can be a dangerous partnership. I remember on one hole midway through the round when Lee teed off and he left it in the right-hand rough for me, while Chris teed off and put Jay in the left-hand bunker.

Jay tried to hit a long iron to the green, caught the lip and rolled back into the bunker; Chris chipped out and then Jay went long. So they were struggling while we were cruising. But you never know in foursomes and sometimes it pays to play clever, even when it looks as if you're sure to win the hole. I've seen so many holes given away stupidly and that's something you just cannot afford to do in the Ryder Cup. The players are so good that you give them an inch and they'll take a long par five.

When my shot from the rough didn't come out very well, I knew it wasn't going to make the green. It eventually finished on a tight pitching surface some 15 yards short. We were there in two and they were through the back in four.

Lee walked ahead because it was going to be his shot. He got to the ball, sized up his options and was about to ask what to do – but I'd already decided for him, because unbeknown to him I'd been in his bag and pulled out the putter, even though he was some distance from the green.

Before his question came out I ripped the cover off the putter head and said, 'This is what you're playing. Get it somewhere on the green, we make five in worst-case scenario, win the hole and move to the next tee.'

At that, he stood aside, laughing at me, but he duly obliged and we won the hole and the match 5&4.

The atmosphere on the Saturday night when we only needed three and a half points to retain the trophy was quietly confident. We had all played well that week and contributed, but we were mindful of what had happened at Brookline so weren't counting our birdies of the chicken variety.

*　　*　　*

It was my fortune to be drawn against Davis in the singles and he had me two down with three to play. The 16th at Oakland Hills is a long, toughish par four with an approach to the green over water. A drive, wedge to 10 feet and birdie putt converted made me one down and still two to go.

The long short-hole 17th is probably the hardest on the course – David Howell would go on to win Shot of the Year from that tee – but I was happy with my first shot. It was a lovely high cut, but I hit it too well and it finished through the green in long rough, while Davis found the trap on the right of the green.

Davis hit a wonderful bunker shot to four feet and I was thinking that somehow I had to get the ball up and down to keep the match alive. I made a good contact and the ball trickled down towards the hole . . . and then unbelievably disappeared.

So we were all square playing the last and after I flushed one straight down the middle, Davis took a driver and pulled it a bit. When he got to his ball Davis called over a referee because it was sitting very close to a sprinkler in the long rough. If he took relief, he'd be able to take a club length and maybe get into the first cut, from where he'd probably get it on to the green. But Davis, being Davis, did not take the drop.

If he had moved his foot one inch further back from his normal stance he would have been standing on the drain and could have taken relief, but in the spirit of the game and the spirit of the Ryder Cup he played the ball where it was. In all my days playing golf, I've never had a greater act of respect shown to me than

Davis did that day. That sums him up perfectly. He is a total and utter gentleman and I have the utmost respect for him.

So Davis had to chop his ball out and couldn't reach the green. I hit a five iron, pushed it a little and ended up just on the wrong side of the hog's back on the green. Davis pitched it up about 12 feet short and then I hit a fairly good putt, considering the difficulty of it, and it rolled on about four feet.

There was no scoreboard to be seen and I had no idea what was going on. Although I had a much easier putt, I said to Davis's caddie, Cubby Burke, 'I'd really like to do good-good here and settle for a half, but I can't see what's happening elsewhere and I don't want to offend Davis by doing the wrong thing. He might want to putt because of the team situation.'

Cubby wasn't sure either, but he said he didn't think I could offer that in the situation, so I said nothing. Davis missing his putt did not make the situation any easier for me. I really did want to offer 'good-good', not just because he's a very good friend, but also because of what he had done in the rough by not taking a drop when it would have been perfectly within his rights to do so. So now I had a gentle right-to-left four-footer to win the match.

I struck a good putt, but it horseshoed out on the low side and I will admit that it was probably the first and last time I have ever been happy to miss a short putt like that. I never thought I would ever feel that way, because the killer instinct dictates you knock it in, win your point and game over. But in my heart of hearts, I was not at all disappointed at missing after what he'd done. It just didn't feel right to win it in those circumstances, but in no way did I not try to hole my putt.

I was perfectly happy with a half and afterwards, while the other players from the two sides gathered in separate groups, Davis, Cubby and I went to the other side of the green, lit up cigars and watched all the other matches finish. Now, that to me is what the Ryder Cup is all about. I'm not saying you should have a cigar, but that was our way of sharing the moment. You play hard, you want to win, but at the end of the day it's a game played between friends.

The one thing European teams are always good at is enjoying themselves – win, lose or draw – and after the win at Oakland Hills it was no different. So when the ladies handed out our evening passes, quite a few of the boys headed for the nearest Irish bar, where Mr Westwood acted as master of ceremonies while standing on the bar introducing all the players.

Our condition when we left the bar was debatable, but Lee, being Lee, was still as sharp as ever . . . and he caught me napping. I was just a couple of strides from a lamp post I had not seen when he shouted, 'Look at that over there.' He knew exactly what he was doing, because while I was trying to figure out what he was talking about, I walked straight into the lamp post and nearly knocked myself out.

Later, back at the hotel, Heather wasn't exactly impressed by my general demeanour. To be honest, she was disgusted, but we had a good trip home and walked straight into a press conference as soon as we landed in Heathrow. This is where the team ethic kicked in again, because whenever a question was asked of me, somebody else would jump in and take it on my behalf. My ability to speak was minimal, so they covered for me splendidly, as good team-mates do.

2006, K Club:
Europe 18½ – 9½ United States

The build-up to the end of qualification for the K Club Ryder Cup coincided with some distressing times in the Clarke household. Heather always wanted me to play, yet although I shot a half-decent first round in the Open at Hoylake, I couldn't break 80 in the second. I missed the cut and decided to suspend my golfing activities indefinitely.

Heather was not at all well, and consequently my mind wasn't in a good place as I was confronted by the press. I was explaining the situation about Heather and why I was not going to play again for the foreseeable future when an American broadcaster chipped in with 'What are you going to do now, Darren? We feel your pain.'

It came across as incredibly patronising. I felt like jumping across and hitting the guy as hard as I possibly could. Instead, I looked over and said, 'That's the most stupid question I've ever been asked.'

I answered a few rather more acceptable questions and then got out of there. To this day, I haven't forgiven him. It was so wrong. It seemed to me that all he was looking for was tears coming out of my eyes. I couldn't then, and I still can't now, see any reason for him to ask that question, except to get a television moment that would make him look good. It felt as if he was trying to take something very serious, something that was life or death, something that was going wrong in my personal life, and use it for his own benefit. It was the lowest of the low.

Heather died a few weeks later and, after everything started to settle down afterwards, I embarked on the process that would eventually lead to my being able to fulfil her last desire of me – to play in the Ryder Cup. I called the captain, Ian Woosnam, and told him simply that if he wanted me to play, I'd be ready. The only reason I made that phone call was because of what Heather had said to me.

My way of dealing with things was to throw myself into practice, and when I'd practised, I'd practise even more. I blocked out everything else and I have to admit I probably wasn't a great father at that stage. Eddie and Alice, our wonderful housekeepers, took the boys to school of a morning and although I picked them up, everything else was practice. The time to grieve and give the boys the attention they deserved would come later. Everything was put on hold except my determination to get into the Ryder Cup team.

Woosie had been non-committal when I'd first called him. He said he would think about it. It must have been a very tough decision, but thankfully he picked me, which took a lot of guts. I was quite a few places down the pecking order after the ten automatic qualifiers. Fair play to him for doing that, because if it hadn't worked out he would have received a lot of stick. People would have reasoned that there was no way I could be ready so soon after Heather's death. He showed a great deal of faith in me and my ability and I was mightily relieved to be able to repay him.

The decision to pick me and Lee Westwood as his wild-card selections was a courageous one, although given our record together, it would have been difficult to select one without the other. It was not universally acclaimed, however, and particularly not by my good friend Thomas Bjørn. Thomas was miffed and to a certain extent I could understand, because he had just missed out on an automatic place and felt his credentials were every bit as strong as mine or Westy's. But it says as much for Thomas as it had for Woosie that the decision did not affect our relationship.

Thank heavens I was picked, because if I hadn't played I'd forever be thinking that I had not been able to grant Heather her wish.

By the time we reached the K Club, I was determined to hold everything together, at least until it was all over. There was a bit of probing by the press for a reaction, but I managed to keep things in check. This was what Heather wanted me to do and I was going to put everything I had into it.

The official functions were difficult because everybody else was with a partner, but the reaction I received was magnificent – and I mean from everybody. Not just the spectators, but also the American team as well as the European team. It is something I will never forget. The caring they showed was unbelievable.

At the end of the day we're one big family out on tour. Everybody knows what's going on in each other's lives, for the most part, and their gestures towards me were very moving that week. None more so than Tiger, and the prying lenses finally got what they'd been hoping for when we met on the practice ground and shared a hug and a few words. It was one of the many moments which tested my ability to hold back the tears that week, but I think I did a pretty good job.

Few showed as much caring and understanding as Phil Mickelson's wife, Amy, who would later be stricken by the same horrible disease that claimed Heather. Amy is a wonderful lady and had always got on well with Heather. As for Phil, although we may have crossed swords a couple of times, I had always respected him as an unbelievable player over a long period. We became much closer here.

European sides seat the players at the opening and closing ceremonies in alphabetical order, whereas the Americans do it in the order of where the players finished in the qualifying process. We file in and out with our wives or partners and alongside a member from the other team. I was across from the Mickelsons and Amy would not have it that I was on my own, so she moved from the wives' side, the outside, into the inside and held both her husband's and my hand.

The two of them were unbelievably wonderful to me all week, but Amy's actions were some of the most moving I encountered. I'm not sure anybody else really noticed what she'd done, but it touched me an awful lot. Phil has become a very good friend, through thick and thin, and I was pleased to be able to offer advice and understanding when they too started going through the painful processes that accompany the fight against cancer.

It seemed a long wait for the opening matches, but the day finally arrived and I had no idea what I was going to do or how I was going to cope. It really was a walk into the unknown, but it turned into one of the most unforgettable experiences of my life and I suspect the same goes for plenty of people who were there to witness it. In fact, it was more a question of hearing it, because I had never heard anything like the noise that greeted me on the first tee that Friday morning, and it would only be rivalled, but not beaten, five years later.

Woosie paired me with Lee – there really wasn't an option – and sent us out last of the morning fourball session because he wanted all the other pairs out on the course and settled down before the eruption he knew was bound to accompany my return to competitive golf for the first time since Heather's death.

I never want to spend too much time on the first tee before a match, but when I was ready to leave the practice green, Lee was still putting and I said, 'Come on, partner, let's go.' But as we walked towards the tee, Lee suddenly ran off and I wondered what on earth he was doing, leaving me in my hour of need.

It wasn't until I turned the corner that I realised why he'd gone ahead. He was working the crowd and, when I came into general view, I was hit by a tsunami of noise. It was unbelievable and all I could do was look up at everybody and nobody and say, 'Thank you.'

We were up against Phil Mickelson and Chris DiMarco and they both gave me a hug and said how pleased they were that I was playing. That showed the true spirit of the Ryder Cup. It's not war; it's a match between friends.

It was written somewhere that I shed a tear on the first tee, but that is incorrect. I just could not afford to let myself go, but somebody thought it would make a better story if they said that I did. I didn't, but Lee and my caddie Billy were shedding them for me at the back of the tee box. In truth, I was in a bit of a daze, and it's probably a good job I didn't see them, otherwise I think I would have broken down as well.

It was my time to hit and I had no idea if I was going to slice it, hook it, push it, pull it, top it or even hit it. It was a surreal moment, because we had moved from deafening noise to being able to hear the flap of a butterfly's wings. Heaven only knows how, but I striped it straight down the middle more than 300 yards. There could never be a harder shot or hole for me to play. Pressure could come no greater.

Billy and Lee were staggered. Billy said he couldn't believe I'd just done what I did, while Lee asked how on earth I'd been able to button it straight down the middle.

I still had 123 yards to the pin and I wasn't sure what was going to happen next. My mind was spinning with thoughts. Don't hit it fat, don't thin it and don't shank it. I hit a wedge to 15 feet. This time I knew exactly what was going to happen. I just knew I would hole the putt. I could close my eyes, look at the crowd, do absolutely anything, but one thing was for sure: the ball was going to drop. I thought, 'Heather's up there watching. It's going in.' It did.

I remember Lee playing wonderfully that morning, but I came in once or twice and most memorably on the last, when a five-wood approach nestled just off the right edge of the green, with the pin middle right, and I putted down to inches for a concession and the win.

Amy was one of the first to give me a hug afterwards, a further illustration of what a great lady she is. I was still in a bit of a daze, but I remember thinking that at least if I did nothing else all competition, I had contributed something and had gone some way to repaying Woosie for the faith he had in me. Thankfully, I was able to do more than that, and I now realise just how wise he was in giving me only two further matches. I could not have coped with more.

Had Woosie asked beforehand, I would have said I wanted to play all five matches, but whatever he decided was fine by me. My next match was against Tiger and Jim Furyk in the Saturday-morning fourball. Woosie knew what he was doing by pairing me with my good mate Lee again. He knew Lee knew Heather and he also knew he would look after me. It's not very often I need taking care of, but that was definitely a time I needed a strong shoulder. Lee was just brilliant all week. There was no real mention of Heather, but he didn't have to because we both knew what the other was thinking. He was there for me and I definitely leant on him. He played fantastic, as he invariably does.

We knew it was going to be tough, but we always seemed to have a handle on the match and although we'd lost the 15th, we were still three up with three to play. On the par-five 16th, we laid up along with Jim, while Tiger hit it over the left-hand trap. As Lee prepared for his shot in, I was willing him to get in a position from which we would have two chances to make birdie. But Lee pushed it and the ball smacked against the rocks and rebounded into water. Only one word went through my head.

I hit my third shot straight down the flag, back shelf left, but it went just over the back of the green. The noise was again deafening as I made my way to the green, unsure of what my lie was and what we'd do if we lost another. Jim was eight feet or so from the hole in three and Tiger wasn't that far away either, so one of them was bound to make birdie. We didn't want to be playing the last having been four up at one stage.

I was mightily relieved to see my ball in a very nice spot. I had a not-too-difficult chip, so I just thought I'd give it a chance and see what happened. It went straight into the hole. Lee went to give me a high five and nearly took my arm off, while Tiger gave me a hug and that was it – 3&2 and two points out of two. With just the singles to go for me, I was so happy to have done my bit, particularly for Woosie.

In the singles, I was drawn against Zach Johnson, and as he said afterwards, 'I didn't feel like I was just playing Darren. I thought I was playing the whole of Ireland.'

The support for me throughout was simply magnificent and the love I felt that week was unprecedented. The compassion that they showed was wonderful and it helped get me through that week. It was always going to be difficult for Zach, even though he is a gutsy competitor, and it didn't help that one or two breaks went my way as well.

I actually looked at the scoreboard on 10 when I went three up and realised that the fate of the Ryder Cup might come down to me. I thought that would just be too much. Nobody could script that.

The truth is, it's not such a big deal who makes the Ryder Cup-winning putt. The press may like to make a big thing about it, but the first point and every other is just as important for the team. When you're out practising on your own, you may think to yourself, 'This is for the Ryder Cup,' but when you are actually in the team situation, it's different. Do the players really care who hits the winning putt? No, just as long as somebody does.

Still, I had to make sure I didn't get ahead of myself, though I knew I was in control of the match. On 12, I was 150 feet from the pin while Zach was just 20 feet away. I wanted him to have to win it and to do that I had to get mine down close. The putt was tracking towards the hole and then broke away, only to break back and, lo and behold, it went straight in the middle and I was four up with just six to play.

My mind started wandering on 13 and I paid the price, and it still wasn't in its correct place on 14, when I putted up to what was a tap-in in my opinion, but Zach wasn't going to give it to me.

I looked at him again and he said, 'All right then, pick it up.' I wasn't intending to be rude by looking at him, but I just wasn't thinking straight.

Three up with four to go, I couldn't help remembering that I had never won a Ryder Cup singles. I thought I had on the 15th, when a putt from 40 feet looked at the hole and decided to stay out. I did not have to wait long, but I was indebted to Zach for a most gracious act on the 16th, never likely to be bettered at a Ryder Cup and at least equal to the occasion when, during a previous Ryder Cup, Jack Nicklaus put his arm around Tony Jacklin's shoulder, gave him a three-footer for a half and said, 'I don't think you'd have missed that, but I didn't want to give you the chance.' That gesture ensured the entire match was halved.

Neither Zach nor I could reach the par five, so after three, I had a 25-foot downhill putt which was fast and left to right. Zach was chipping, but from closer, so it was all to play for, and if I was thinking anything, it certainly wasn't straight. I left my putt two feet short and as Zach walked by me he said, 'I can't give you that, Darren.' That was fine by me. He almost made his chip, so now I had my putt for the match and I had no idea how I was going to get the ball in the hole. My head was spinning and I honestly did not think I would be able to pull the putter back and then hit.

Zach may or may not have realised my predicament, but he obviously decided he did not want to put me through any more turmoil and extremely generously gave me the putt. What a magnanimous gesture and one I will never forget.

We hugged and then I turned to Billy and just couldn't hold back any more. I was a mess as a flood of emotions took over. The Thames Barrier could not have stopped them.

Woosie was all teary as well and he said, 'It's destiny.'

I was just so thankful I had not let him down. Tom Lehman came over and said some very special words, as did Tiger shortly afterwards, and then Mum, Dad and Andrea came for a family hug.

I soon discovered that it was Henrik Stenson's point that had decided the match and that was fine by me. Europe had won and that was all that mattered.

For the closing ceremony we all wore our pink jackets and it was only when I was donning mine for the first time that I twigged its relevance - the breast cancer-awareness colour. When Woosie dedicated the Ryder Cup to Heather, I doubt there was a dry eye in the house.

Heather had wanted me to play and I'd done my bit. I knew she would have been proud.

2008, Valhalla:
United States 16½ – 11½ Europe

It was America's turn to host the next series of matches and Europe would have Nick Faldo, now Sir Nick, at the helm.

There are very difficult decisions to be made in terms of wild-card selections and Nick not picking me for one was disappointing. He'd said in the build-up that he'd wanted guys in form and I had not only won earlier in the season at the BMW Asian Open, but also two weeks before the selection process was completed, at the KLM Open. I was enjoying a rich vein of form. Obviously it wasn't rich enough, but the captain has to pick what he thinks is the best team.

Relying on a wild card to get in the team has a message to it – play better so that you don't need one next time. You can really have no qualms whatsoever if you don't get a pick. I understand these things a lot more now than I did then, because I am older and arguably wiser.

2010, Celtic Manor:
Europe 14½ – 13½ United States

I did get selected for Celtic Manor, but not for the team. I was needed to help in the team room and I had no hesitation in agreeing when Colin Montgomerie asked me to be one of his vice-captains. It was an honour I am privileged to have been able to perform and an experience I shall be able to draw on should the powers that be ever decide I am a suitable candidate for the captaincy.

Monty was incredibly thorough and a wonderful captain throughout. He had his own opinions, but he wanted everybody else's and was always open to suggestions. The playing talisman for so long, he had always been the team leader on the course. The same determination, desire and winning mentality came through in his captaincy. Like Seve, he would refuse to be beaten.

I have nothing but the highest praise for him in that wet week in Wales. All the vice-captains had good meetings with him and we weren't shy of voicing our opinions. He listened to and digested everything we said and then went with his own gut instinct. You can have all the opinions and information, but you have to make the call yourself when you are the captain . . . and that's what he did.

It was another of those Ryder Cups where Europe had a good lead going into the last session, but America had shown through history that they were traditionally stronger in the singles. Here would be no exception, and it all came down to the last match, between my good friend Graeme McDowell and Hunter Mahan.

Graeme won on the 17th and the scenes that followed were fitting for what was a magnificent competition between evenly-matched teams.

I did enjoy it, but for me it was a strange situation afterwards. When G-Mac won, I thought that's it, I'm done. I had been part of the back-up team, but I hadn't been part of the playing team and I didn't feel comfortable, so I had a couple of pints and then went to bed. I had been there to assist in every way I could, but when it was over, it wasn't for me, because the glory was for others. This stage now belonged to Monty and the players.

One thing about being on the sidelines and watching from outside is that it's stoked my feeling about being good enough to play in at least one more. It did not quite happen in 2012 but I was honoured again to be an assistant to Jose Maria Olazabal and the team at Medinah. Yet I have a wonderful role model in Miguel Angel Jiménez, who is five years older than me and still performing week in, week out. Another Ryder Cup, even at 45 and probably older, is not beyond me.

Maybe winning the Open also strengthened my credentials for being Ryder Cup captain one day, because being a major champion does earn you a little more respect from players. As to when that will be, if at all, that is down to the committee, but it is definitely an ambition.

I'd like to think that I can still contend for a place in 2014. So we will see. That's when it goes to Scotland and Gleneagles, somewhere I've made some disparaging remarks about in the past. But that won't get in the way of my desire to get in the team.

When it comes to my views – and I mean about everything, not just Gleneagles – they're quite straightforward. To me, a spade is a spade and I'll say what I think. That may not be to some people's liking, but I've always done it.

Anyway, I'm sure the Ryder Cup in 2014 will be a fantastic event, as it has been for numerous years now. We will see how things work out and whatever role, if any, I have in it, I will be delighted to be there.

11

COACHES AND CADDIES

Coaches

There are few top coaches, of either the swing or mental variety, that I haven't seen at one stage or another. I'm sure they find me very trying, but I am inquisitive by nature and I always want to know how things work and how I can improve.

The problem with my mental side is that it's like a yo-yo. Sometimes it's good, sometimes it's bad; sometimes it's excellent and sometimes it's terrible. There is no consistency. I first decided to seek advice on this aspect of the game when I was just 16, which was way before the vast majority of golfers on the Tour considered tapping into that sort of thing. But from the moment in my early teens when I knew I wanted to be a professional golfer I was committed to the game, and I was happy to drink from any well that I thought would benefit my ambitions.

It was **Peter Dennison** who helped me early on. He is simply wonderful: old-school, different, bordering on eccentric, but a very clever and astute man. He has seen me through thick and thin and I can't speak too highly of him. One thing is for sure, I definitely would not be where I am today without his help, and twenty-odd years down the line I still see him now and again.

There is no stereotype for sports psychologists and I must say that of the multitude I have seen no two are alike. Certainly very few are anything like **Jos Vanstiphout**. The diminutive Belgian is a one-off. He first came to prominence through his work with Retief Goosen, and many other top golfers, including fellow US Open winners Ernie Els and Michael Campbell, have used his services.

Most psychologists are softly spoken and very measured in their attitude. Not Jos, who has no formal training as a psychologist but is an ardent reader of the science. He leads with his chin and occasionally adopts a fairly aggressive stance, snapping and snarling rather than treading lightly. It seems to work for some people. Not with me, unfortunately. I was working with Jos when I shot that 60 at the K Club, but it was to no avail as I eventually lost a big lead to Lee Westwood – a defeat which left its mental scars for some time afterwards.

I've usually managed to glean something helpful from those whose job it is to help others realise their potential. I was fortunate to be able to collaborate on a book with **Dr Karl Morris** and I still refer to *Golf: The Mind Factor* when I need to remind myself of his teachings. I am also indebted to **Mike Finnigan**, CEO of i2i Sports, who has been very helpful in educating me about the psychological strategies leading to success, but the man I most often turn to in times of mental turmoil is American sports psychologist and author **Dr Bob Rotella**, arguably the world's most renowned practitioner of the art. The beauty of Dr Bob is the plain and simple way he puts over his message, and there can be no doubt he was key to my eventual major success at Royal St George's.

And then of course there is the amateur psychologist to beat all amateur psychologists – Chubby. His tips have mostly been delivered late at night when we have had a couple of halves of shandy. But joking apart, he's always wanted the best for me. He's seen my career develop through the good times and bad times and he's always been there with a word of wisdom. Whether he's been right is another matter, but he's always thought he was.

It's been a similar story on the swing side. I've been to most of the top swing coaches down the years.

With Ireland training camps it was initially **John Garner**, a former Tour player who was all p's and s's – past the flag, short of the flag. Nowadays you don't always need to be past the flag, but back then that was his mantra whenever we had country coaching sessions in Malone or Dublin. Then it changed to **Howard Bennett**, whose brain I picked on a few occasions, but after I turned professional I went straight to **Bob Torrance**.

Bob, father of Sam, is a wonderful man with a heart as big as a huge haggis and an accent as thick as porridge, though coming from Northern Ireland, where such noises were not uncommon, I was able to understand him better than most. I had some great times in Largs over the years. You get coached by Bob and end up being part of the family.

Bob's teachings were Hogan, Hogan, Hogan, which wasn't a bad thing considering the American legend was widely considered to have had the best swing in the game during his time. Bob would look for a little rotation of the left forearm and getting into the position which allowed you to hit as hard as you wanted. I spent many a horrible day in the freezing cold searching for secrets, and Bob and his equally lovely wife June looked after me for years and years.

After we'd finished on the range and defrosted we'd always go for a couple of pints down in Largs and when we came back June would have dinner ready. We'd tuck into a hearty meal and then watch a video of what we'd been doing. Bob would fall asleep on the sofa, then I'd fall asleep and June would come through and shout at both of us to go to bed. They were and still are brilliant people and they were very happy times.

Bob was unbelievably supportive. It was very hard when I decided it was time for me to move on. Having to tell Bob that I wanted to go somewhere else was one of the most awkward things I have ever had to do in my career. I felt I was letting him down. It hurt me to have to do it, but I felt I had to.

I saw **David Leadbetter** a couple of times and liked what he said, but my next close association would be with somebody who might seem a less likely recipient of my coaching affections. **Pete Cowen** is a dour Yorkshireman, full of dry humour and regimental in his ways, which include taking his favourite brand of breakfast tea with him when travelling abroad.

There is nothing Pete doesn't know about the swing, having dismantled and reconstructed hundreds of them. He has had immense faith in me over the years throughout our relationship

abe in arms: with Dad aged six months.

Liverpool fan: aged eight.

roud parents Hetty and Godfrey and my
nior Ireland blazer.

Blue is the colour.

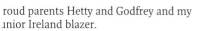

Above: Well done, sis: Dungannon club captain Peter Dolan in 1985 handing over the Traders Cup to Andrea and me.

Left: Coach Bob Torrance looks on at Royal Portrush in 1994.

eady for lift-off: with Stephen Boler, Wayne Westner, Peter Bucksey (pilot) and hubby Chandler.

.ome from home at South Africa's Sun City in 2005.

Above: Preparing a wedding toast to cousin Lesley Patterson in Donegal.

Left: The bells were ringing for Heather and me in March 1996.

Below: Andrea and Davy marry in 1996.

nxious times for captain Seve Ballesteros
t the Valderrama Ryder Cup in 1997.

Ryder rookie: making my cup debut at
Valderrama.

Vinners all: the 1997 Ryder Cup team.

Winning trio: with Heather and Tyrone after victory in the 1998 Volvo Masters at Jerez.

Preparing for the Battle of Brookline in 1999: watched by coach Butch Harmon, caddie Billy Foster and Chubby.

ast-day red: Tiger during our WGC Match lay final at La Costa in 2000.

On the way to victory against Tiger at La Costa, my first WGC win.

umping for joy: Paul McGinley celebrates ne putt that guaranteed Europe's win in ne 2002 Ryder Cup at the Belfry.

Two Torrances: Captain Sam and father Bob enjoy our 2002 win.

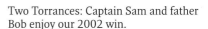

Family guy: with Conor, Tyrone and Heather at Sunningdale in 2002.

Team Liverpool: with Conor and Tyrone and their cousins Callum and Chris.

and I was delighted to be able to repay him through winning at Royal St George's.

Pete has had to talk me down from the shelf on many an occasion and has always believed in me, always known my capabilities and been a huge supporter, so it was nice, after all the years of work we have done together, to win and actually give a bit of pleasure back.

We've had our rows and disagreements about what's going on with my swing, as is common between coach and player. He's more often than not dressed in black from tip to toe and you always know when he's deep in thought because you'll see him standing on the range with his left hand cupping his right elbow and his right hand stroking his moustache.

His knowledge is unquestionable, but it has also caused its problems between the two of us. I'm not very technical – it's just not my angle – and sometimes the way Pete used to put across his thoughts would lose me. I'm more a 'do this, do that and carry on' player, but Pete always wanted to help me so much he'd go down the technical side or any other if he thought it meant I'd improve.

Whatever our past differences, I love him to bits. He's absolutely fantastic and I don't know anybody on the planet who works harder than he does. He does everything for his family and he's an unbelievably good, genuine, trustworthy man.

I've also spent a lot of time with former Tour player turned television pundit and part-time coach **Ewen Murray**, who is not only a very wise man, but also like a big brother to me. We have similar passions in fly fishing and fine red wine and we've had some great times at Queenwood at the back of the range with a nice bottle. The two things I miss from living near London are Ewen and **Keith Maxwell**, at Sunningdale, because both of them have helped me on the golf course and off it.

I've never been shy of asking advice and questions of others. Be it Seve, Greg, Nick, Sandy, Woosy, Bernhard, Ollie or Uncle Tom Cobley – if I've thought I might benefit from their words of wisdom, then I have never been afraid to ask them. And I've always written down the things I thought helpful and important in my little black book. It's a great reference book, which I go back to a lot.

The point I'm making is that the people I have gone to have generally been older and often wiser. And off the course the guys I would class as my confidants are also older – Chubby, Maxy, Pete and Ewen being the principal ones. There is no substitute for experience, so I've always surrounded myself with people who are more intelligent than myself and who will give me a straight answer. I don't want yes-men and I've been fortunate in having a lot of wise guys around me. I learn from them not only in golf things, but other aspects of life too.

They don't come much more experienced than **Butch Harmon**. Both in golf and life, he's been there and done it quite a few times. I had a great time with Butch and British coach **Wayne Johnson**, now in Dubai, when I used to go to see them at their Rio Secco base in Las Vegas. It was there that my friendship with Tiger developed, because he would often be there when I visited.

The beauty of Butch is in his simplicity. There is nothing complicated in his teachings and he is so untechnical. He still follows my progress via the Golf Channel and he will tell me the same things now that he did then, because we still speak frequently. Early this year I was hitting balls in Dubai and catching up with Wayne when Butch came on the phone to him. Wayne happened to say I was there and Butch immediately told him a couple of things to check with my swing and putting stroke to ensure I hadn't slipped back into bad habits.

Butch is golf through and through and has an abundance of stories which never fail to entertain. We'd often stand there on the range, have a chat and share a joke as if it was just another day of practice, when in reality it was immediately before the last round of a major. He definitely knows how to put a player at ease, whatever the day or occasion. He'd take all the pressure away and then tell me to go out and play.

The great thing for me is that I am still on very good terms with those who have coached me over the years. We're still friends and I think that some of that comes from me always confronting things. When it comes to coaches and caddies and having to move on sometimes, for the most part I've done it face to face. To some extent, I think that's why I've retained a good relationship with them.

Caddies

I've had far more caddies than coaches and they are an equally remarkable breed. The old image of scruffily-attired drunks who look as if they have been dragged through a hawthorn bush backwards is way out of date now. Not many, if any, would claim to be anywhere near teetotal, but there are far more ripped bodies than beer bellies these days, and the vast majority are clean, tidy and professional. The rewards are too great for any other approach.

The things I demand of a caddie include being as hard-working as me, never being late, being prepared to stay longer than anyone else, supportive when I'm down and knowing when to speak and when not to. I don't mean that in a derogatory way, but there are times on the golf course when a caddie has to know when to pipe up and when to keep his mouth firmly closed. Those who have embraced these demands have been properly rewarded.

I've tested the resolve and patience of all shapes and sizes, but all have been well looked after if they have looked after me. **Gary Johnson** from Dungannon was followed by my first professional caddie **Richard**, who, if he had a surname I was never aware of it, but he hadn't been on the Tour long, and then came **Barry the Judge**, a very good caddie and now sadly passed away. He left me, it happens, for Anders Forsbrand, who I think he'd caddied for at the Dunhill Cup at St Andrews and did well with so decided to stay on.

Then came the incomparable Rowley, who in my affectionate opinion can only be described as different. **Martin Rowley** came to caddying via the bar, and not the one associated with judges and chambers.

One Sunday we were playing up at Mas Nou in Catalonia and I'd shot six under on the front nine and caught up with the leaders, who were just teeing off. By the 13th hole I was beginning to feel rather nervous because I was in the lead and when we got on the tee, I asked Rowley for a cigarette. I was thinking that if I could make a couple more birdies and get safely into the clubhouse, then I might have a chance.

Rowley gave me a cigarette but he'd lost his lighter, so all he had was a box of matches. He somehow managed to light a match, but his hands were shaking so much he couldn't get it to the end of the cigarette. I thought, 'For heaven's sake, Rowley, if I'm nervous, I need you not to be. You're supposed to be the Tour caddie and your hands are shaking that much you can't light a cigarette.' I didn't win the tournament.

A few weeks later I shocked him at Monte Carlo. It wasn't the first of my two Tour 60s that surprised him, so much as the fact that at the end of the week I sacked him. He couldn't believe it, especially after such a low score, but I'd already made my mind up that a parting of the ways was inevitable.

Not that I didn't see him after that often enough. Rowley could smell a new batch of outfits arriving at my house from five miles away and would suddenly turn up on the doorstep enquiring about what I'd be doing with the clothes I wouldn't be needing any more. They invariably found their way on to his back.

After trying a succession of caddies I then started a partnership that lasted more than ten years. Player-caddie relationships can be difficult. I've had some very, very good ones, but if you don't completely hit it off it's tough. You spend so much time together that eventually you're going to annoy them or they're going to annoy you. Fortunately, I hit it off straight away with **Billy Foster**, who had served a tough apprenticeship with some of golf's most volatile characters. It seemed a perfect fit for me and that's how it panned out.

I think Billy had finished with Seve not long before and David Grice from Fairway Travel got us together for the Irish Open at Mount Juliet in July 1995. He embraces all the qualities needed to satisfy my high professional standards while being good company and funny in a sarcastic kind of way.

Billy was particularly strong if he was convinced I was asking for the wrong club. There were two occasions, at Carnoustie and Hilton Head in South Carolina, where I wanted to hit a driver and Billy was adamant it was a three wood.

'Driver, Billy,' I said.

'No, three wood,' he replied.

'Give me the driver.'

'No.'

'Give me the ******* driver.'

I think he got his way at Carnoustie, but I wrestled the driver off him at Hilton Head and promptly put the ball into the water. I could have sworn I saw a little smile in the corner of his mouth, but he quickly disguised it.

We became very close, which wasn't difficult because he is a proper guy. We went through some hard times in our personal lives together. He's just a genuine all-round fantastic guy – somebody that I would trust with my life.

We had an excellent working relationship, but it sadly ended the year after Heather passed away. I wasn't coping too well with the situation and he wasn't making any money. He wrote me a letter and then called me. In a tearful conversation he explained why he had to move on and I totally understood. He left to work on a job share with Sergio, before finally getting sacked himself and moving on to Lee Westwood. I really do hope they win a major together. I can't think of two more deserving people.

Other caddies came and went and then I teamed up with **Phil Morbey**, commonly known as Wobbly for his gait and best known for being with Ian Woosnam for many years. Like Billy, Wobbly is a Yorkshireman and consequently not frightened of voicing his opinions. He has a bit of a fiery temperament and something of a loud mouth now and again, but that's part and parcel of him and it's all good fun. As a caddie, like Billy, he is the ultimate professional.

Our temperaments were going to clash at some point, however, and it came at the Honda Classic in West Palm Beach in 2009. I was cruising and not far off the lead, but bogeyed 16 and trebled 17 after hitting out of a bunker into a pond, so I was well and truly snared in the Bear Trap, as the closing holes of Jack Nicklaus's design are known. By the time I stood on the 18th tee my mind was delicate, to say the least. This was an occasion when the caddie should know when to keep quiet and when to speak up.

I hit a good shot off the tee and I asked Wobbly what to hit for my lay-up. He gave me a lay-up yardage to the bunker and I said four iron, but he said five was plenty. I went with his recommendation and he kept quiet. I turned it over on the breeze a little and then never saw it finish. I asked Wobbly where it was, because I thought it was bound for the semi-rough. He said he didn't know, so I asked if it was in the bunker and he repeated that he didn't know. I was at boiling point because of the previous dropped shots, so you can imagine what I felt like when I found it in the bunker.

Apparently, I'd made Wobbly fume because, within his hearing, I'd gone over to the other caddie and asked what they'd hit for their lay-up. Anyway, I made a par five and when I came out from signing my card I said to him, 'What the hell did you lay me up in the bunker for?' He just said he didn't do it on purpose, and that the ball had only just made the bunker and it was in a position where we could get to the green.

It's what he said next that sent me over the edge: 'Good job we didn't hit four iron then, because you'd have been up against the face and not been able to get to the green.' That was enough and it prompted a shouting match across the putting green 30 yards apart. He headed off, saying, 'If you want me to work for you tomorrow, call me.'

I thought, 'I'm not calling you. You turn up for work; it's your job.'

I didn't call him, he didn't call me and he didn't show up the following day. For a couple of days I thought he was a bit of a twit, or something not quite as pleasant, but after that we were OK again, although I did need a new caddie.

J.P. Fitzgerald, who has had a few good bags and is currently with Rory McIlroy - nice work if you can get it - was also with me for a time, although I knew him more not for being a caddie, but for beating me in the semi-final of the Irish Amateur back in 1989. He had something like 21 putts for 18 holes, but when they picked the Irish team immediately afterwards, I was included and he wasn't, which just goes to show you never know in golf.

As a caddie he was very good both on and off the course and we were together in 2003 when I won my second WGC event at Firestone. J.P. knew my game inside out. He was very much into statistics and always kept an eye on things, checking which areas I might need to work on more than others. He was never scared to speak his mind and that's an important quality, but as well as being good company on the course he was equally agreeable company on the road. An important thing about a caddie is that you're able to spend some time together when travelling, and we frequently had too many drinks in each other's company.

One of those occasions followed that WGC win. After the ceremony, press and handshakes, we flew up to Providence, Rhode Island, and found a very quiet Irish bar and sat in a corner minding our own business. I doubt that there is a bar in America which doesn't have at least one television somewhere and this one was no different. The big screen showed American football and then baseball - and then the highlights of the golf.

The barman looked at me, looked at the television, looked back at me, looked at the television and said, 'Is that you?'

There were four or five people in the pub at that stage, but within an hour it was standing-room only. It was Labor Day Weekend that week, so the next tournament didn't start until the following Friday. It didn't take us long to realise we didn't have to be too careful about intake because we had an extra day to get over whatever hangover was coming our way. It was four in the morning by the time we finally made our way out of the building, and that was after I'd been accidentally pushed on to the floor while people danced all around me as I tried to regain my balance and senses. It took a while.

Of all the people who have helped me through the years, it would be remiss of me not to mention **John 'Newt the Beaut' Newton**. Newt spent the best part of ten years not just travelling with me but unpacking my bags, repacking them, stretching me to aid flexibility, taking the mickey and generally making sure I had everything I needed.

Big John, as he is also called, was once a bodyguard for Miss World and was always full of good humour. Like us all, he also had his idiosyncrasies and his was to bring back all the free magazines available at supermarkets throughout the world detailing local house prices. Don't ask me.

Newt's help and companionship were much appreciated.

One of the most ironic caddie stories came from the build-up to the 2011 Open and it involved one of the longest-serving and most notable practitioners of that particular trade. **Ricci Roberts** has been through several marriages and divorces with South African living legend Ernie Els during their successful time together and was in divorce mode when I needed somebody to get me back into the swing of things.

Ricci, or No 1 as he is known in the caddie shack, agreed to come with me and we were settling into a reasonable understanding and working relationship when I had a terrible weekend in Morocco after going into it close to the lead and playing well. My form over the last two rounds could not be attributed in any way to Ricci, but I was on the verge of quitting again.

I was due to go to the Far East afterwards, but I was not in the right frame of mind and Chubby told me just to get away from the game for a few weeks, take a rest and come back refreshed. I cleared my head in the Bahamas for three weeks and texted Ricci on the way back to tell him I'd see him in Mallorca for the Iberdrola Open.

I got a text back asking if Chubby hadn't told me that he was going to Ernie's induction into the Hall of Fame. I said I didn't know, but not to worry because ISM would find me somebody. That somebody was the very experienced **John Mulrooney**, who would go on to be my caddie at Royal St George's.

12

HEATHER

I met Heather Tosh in Kelly's Nightclub in Portrush on a date set up by somebody I can't remember, but I have a lot to thank them for.

It was in the days when smoking was still allowed inside public establishments and I accidentally dropped a cigarette on her brand-new leather jacket. I certainly know how to charm a girl. I said don't worry, I'll buy you another. Anyway, I must have made some kind of more acceptable impression because I was due on a television programme the following weekend in Dublin and she accepted my invitation to accompany me.

The first thing that struck me about Heather, who was working as a rep for a hairdressers travelling around Ireland selling products into salons, was her good looks. She got my sense of humour, most of the time, and we started getting on really well and that developed into love. We did have our share of rows, because she was almost as headstrong as I was, but we were a good match. She let me get away with very little and always stood her ground, which was exactly what I admired and needed. Her strong character was another huge plus and she would always stand up for what she believed in. She didn't suffer fools gladly and her first impressions were invariably correct.

I proposed a year after we first met and we were married exactly a year after that. She'd lost her father at a young age, but her mother, Anne, still lives in Portrush and sees the boys regularly, which I think is important. We were married – Brian Smith, who had caddied for me a bit in the early days, was best man – in Ballywillan Presbyterian Church, Portrush and then had our reception in the Galgorm Manor in Ballymena. As far as I can remember, I didn't do anything stupid like standing on her toes or anything, and then we went to the Maldives for our honeymoon.

When Tyrone was born, in 1998, in Ballymoney, the responsibilities of parenthood weighed far more on Heather's shoulders than on mine for the simple reason that I spent so much time away from home. Frequent absenteeism came with the territory and she understood completely. Not that I was a totally neglectful father. I tried to do my share of night-time feeds and nappy changes when I was back home. I found it incredibly hard to get up every three hours to perform the duties that all parents have to, but at least I knew that I would be getting some sleep again when I was out on the road. Conor came along in 2000 – about six months after we'd moved to London.

Heather was always very independent, but she agreed that it would be easier for me to commute around the world from London than it was from Northern Ireland. We also agreed that it may be a safer place in which to raise our children. Heather grew up in the middle of the Troubles, as I did, and I didn't want my kids growing up in the same environment.

Manchester was an option because the ISM offices are just outside the city, but on balance we felt somewhere closer to London would be easier, even though we knew very few people there. We opted for Sunningdale. Paul McGinley had a word in the right ears and I was allowed to play on Sunningdale golf club's excellent courses . . . becoming very good friends with the professional, Keith Maxwell, at the same time. Unexpectedly, we would also become next-door neighbours to Paul and his wife, Ali – buying houses that backed on to one another without knowing it.

Unfortunately the move would not be as successful for our Pyrenean mountain dog Banbha, who was soon to find out that although she was named after the Irish goddess of sovereignty, that sovereignty did not extend to Sunningdale. Our grounds weren't very extensive and during the period where Banbha was marking out her territory, one of the neighbours reported her for barking too much.

That was pretty upsetting and our first thought was 'What a bunch of ******* we've moved in next to' – though we weren't referring to the McGinleys, who were extremely good friends, especially during Heather's illness. It had been a big step for my wife to move with a young child, but Ali could not have been better or kinder to her. In the end, Banbha was rehomed in Kildare, where she could bark away without a care or complaint in the world.

The next move, in the early summer of 2002, was not as agreeable – at least initially. I was determined to have a bigger house and grounds, and that's exactly what I got, because it was 12,000 square feet with 13 acres. Heather was against Longcross from the start. She felt she'd be isolated in a big property, but the bonus for me was that the house was fairly secure on all sides and was just one minute away from Queenwood, a private course which was ideal for my golfing needs.

I left everything regarding decor, furniture and so on to Heather. Every wall was sponge-painted by hand and after about two months it was just about done. If Heather had been apprehensive about moving there, her fears were quickly confirmed when the entire underfloor heating system packed in. There was only one thing we could do. As all the floors were ripped up, we moved out, the workmen came back in to replace the system and reconcrete the floor and then the decorators had to redo all the paintwork. What a nightmare, as Heather reminded me, 'I told you so.'

We did have some good times in the house after that, though, and there was plenty of room for the kids to do whatever they wanted, so they enjoyed it. They went to school at nearby Coworth Park, and then Tyrone started at Papplewick, in Windsor. They were both excellent schools, but boarding was mandatory at Papplewick at a certain age and that was something we had some reservations about.

Our concerns about boarding were trailing in last by a distance when during the Christmas of 2001 Heather discovered something that would ultimately claim her life and change the lives of all those close to her.

We were in Northern Ireland for the holidays and Heather mentioned on Boxing Day that a lump in her left breast was sore, which was unusual from what we were told later. Soreness was not a common partner for the early form of breast cancer. We went to see a specialist in Coleraine, who recommended we have it looked into further.

We flew back to London in early January and saw another specialist, who conducted a series of biopsies. The news was not good, but the diagnosis was not as bad as we feared. Heather had a form of breast cancer called DCIS – ductal carcinoma in situ – which we were told is the most common type of non-invasive breast cancer. The chances of her dying from it were one in 10,000. Heather was to become the one.

When anything happens that I don't understand, I immediately want to know as much as I can about cause, cure, treatment and what is likely to happen. We were told that the 'ductal' meant that the cancer had started inside the milk ducts, the 'carcinoma' referred to any cancer that begins in the skin or other tissues that line internal organs, and the 'in situ' referred to where it first formed.

We were told that DCIS was not aggressively life-threatening, but it could increase the chances of developing a secondary invasive strain at some later point. If there was to be a recurrence, it would probably be between five and ten years after the original diagnosis, but the chances of it recurring were under 30 per cent.

Our initial feelings were, I'm sure, the same as anybody else's in that predicament, and mostly centred on worry and fear. The kids didn't know what was happening because at that stage they were too young to understand. One thing we knew was that Heather's mum, Anne, had also had the same disease several years back and was still going strong.

Whatever it took, was how we faced it and Heather began the most courageous battle anybody could have fought. She was unbelievably brave.

We were encouraged by the very high survival rate. A few days later Heather had a mastectomy and the specialist was confident that would be the end of it. It was – for then and a couple of years afterwards.

Early in 2004 Heather started complaining about having a sore chest and difficulty swallowing. She didn't make a big deal of it but went to see the doctor, who treated her for whatever he thought it was. As the year went on the problem got worse and worse, but I never knew, simply because she kept it from me. It was the year of the Oakland Hills Ryder Cup and she didn't want to bother me with her problems. She wouldn't tell me how bad she was feeling and I only learned about it the following October when she couldn't put up with it any more.

We went to our local GP and Heather was sent for a scan. As soon as the results came in, the doctor called and said he would like to see the two of us the following Saturday morning. When the doctor asks to see both of you, you know. We anticipated what was coming, but you still can't prepare for it, because you just don't want to hear it.

'Heather,' he said, 'I'm sorry; your breast cancer has come back.'

After thinking she'd come through it, had got rid of it and would be fine again, there she was facing secondary breast cancer, and we both knew that that has a very high mortality rate.

We were stunned. Our heads went into a spin. Our entire world went upside down. There was a wave of questions. What are we going to do? How are we going to deal with this? What's the way forward?

When it comes to health issues, I switch into a very pragmatic mode. Right, what can we do? What options do we have? Write them all down. Figure them all out. Who can we see? Who's the best?

Having been relatively successful in my chosen profession, I was in the very fortunate position of having lots of different options, so after a few days weighing everything up we went to see Heather's oncologist, a wonderful man called Dr Steve Johnston at the Royal Marsden Hospital in London. We went to see him in Fulham – he practised both there and at the other Royal Marsden in Sutton on the outskirts of the capital.

Heather went on a pretty intensive course of different drugs and medicines. It was always a case of hoping for the best, praying for a good set of blood results, searching for any good signs at all. But there was none. Things went progressively downhill from there, yet she always had a positive outlook on things.

I remember on one occasion she had gone into the Fulham hospital for a few scans and an overnight stay and Ellen Maxwell, Keith's wife, and Ali McGinley came to visit and brought her a couple of half bottles of champagne. When I went to see her later she was having a cigarette out of the window with a glass of champagne in her hand – that was Heather.

Our relationship had been somewhat strained before she got ill the second time. All couples go through good times and bad times, but we hadn't been reading from the same page. Heather's illness changed everything.

When Dr Steve told us about the returned cancer he could not have been more positive or truthful. He told us how he had a patient now almost six years into her secondary, so it wasn't all doom and gloom. I cannot speak too highly of him. He was a man of similar age to me who had two young kids and had actually lost his own wife to breast cancer. To be doing what he did having gone through exactly the same thing himself enabled him to see all the parallels. He understood and I felt closer to him because of it.

One of the things I loved about Heather was that she was totally unselfish. Here I was in a sport where I had to be selfish, and there she was going through the worst thing imaginable, without one thought for her own predicament.

She didn't want me worrying about her when I had to concentrate on what I was doing. She wanted me to compete, so her thoughts were on me and her kids, and she felt that if I did well, then the kids would be OK. So she kept an awful lot from me.

Me being me, I made it very clear to Steve that I wanted to know everything; he hadn't to keep anything from me. I wanted to know more than he probably wanted to tell us, but he was very frank and told me what he thought.

*   *   *

Things took a further turn for the worse during the 2006 PGA Championship at Wentworth. It was the week Liverpool won the Champions League after being 3-0 down. Heather had gone into hospital because she wasn't feeling well and her heart was having difficulty coping with the new medication she was taking. We had known that this was a possible side effect and unfortunately our fears were realised.

Although Heather was sick, she wasn't that bad and she encouraged me to keep practising because she wanted me to play in the tournament. We'd also invited an assortment of players, caddies, officials and colleagues to a barbecue at the house and I made sure they were well looked after before setting off for the hospital again. I turned on the television in her room at the hospital to watch the greatest Champions League comeback of all time. There I was shouting at the television, with Heather laughing at me.

I played half decent for two rounds of the PGA, but there was a message waiting for me after the second day to say that Heather's condition had deteriorated and she had been transferred to another hospital, where they'd put a stent into her heart to keep it going again. I immediately withdrew from the tournament and went to the hospital.

It was touch-and-go for a time and it was obvious she was close to dying. The side effects of the new drugs were horrific, but being the fighter she was Heather eventually pulled through.

When Heather finally came out of hospital, she was put on steroids to help her cope with some of the drugs and those had their own side effects. She was starting to retain fluids and her face blew up, but she wasn't going to stay at home and feel sorry for herself. Instead she went with Ali and Michelle Lineker on a girls' trip to the South of France and had a good time.

When the Open at Hoylake came round in the middle of July my mind was anywhere but on the golf course. After shooting a second-round 82 and missing the cut, I took the decision that however much Heather encouraged me to keep going, I would not play again for the foreseeable future.

It was shortly after Heather came back from her French trip that we discovered that the cancer had spread into her spine and she couldn't get about. Very soon she couldn't walk, so I thought I'd buy her one of those single-seater, four-wheeled motorised mobility scooters so she could at least get out and about.

Heather was such a proud lady and she took one look at her new mode of transport, turned to me and said, 'You know exactly where you can shove that. The last thing I will ever do in this world is get on that thing.' Whatever she was losing, it certainly wasn't her pride.

Things were now getting to a pretty desperate state, but we were not giving up. Steve told us about the University of Texas MD Anderson Cancer Center, one of the world's foremost research and treatment clinics, where they were then doing clinical trials with new drugs.

We packed our bags and headed to Houston, but before they could treat her they had to do some tests to see if she was strong enough to have the treatment. She wasn't. Heather was still up and about when we went to Houston, but they were only prepared to test the drugs on people who had a certain degree of health and Heather's heart was not up to the task.

Going through cancer as we had, you always have to have hope, but going there and coming back with the realisation that we were approaching the end was truly awful. It was a very long journey home. We had run out of options. And still she did not complain.

However, Heather was getting progressively worse. She knew it, I knew it and Steve told us so, but we weren't just going to sit about and wait for the inevitable. We wanted to have one last holiday with the kids, and at that time travelling wasn't too big an issue because we had the jet I shared with Lee Westwood.

Somebody found us a beautiful villa in Greece where we could go, but I stressed it had to be wheelchair-friendly, because by this time Heather had no power in her legs and consequently could not walk. We took a four-hour flight from Farnborough to Greece, then the pilots dropped us off and headed back to London. We were just forty-five minutes from the villa, but as soon as we got there we realised it was not in the least bit wheelchair-friendly. There were steps everywhere and it would have been impossible.

By the time the pilots got to Farnborough there was a message for them to fly straight back to Greece and pick us up again. Meanwhile the ever-dependable Sarah Harris, Chubby's PA and ISM's office manager, had found us somewhere ideal in Portugal, so that's where we headed to.

But Heather was not doing well. Her condition got worse and she was taken to a Portuguese hospital, where they stabilised her, but the doctors would not let her move or do anything. We couldn't take her home in the jet; it had to be an air ambulance. We just could not comprehend how busy air ambulances are, but Sarah eventually found one.

The boys were very upset when the paramedics came to collect their mother, but we couldn't all go together, so Heather's mum flew with her while I took the boys back in the jet. It was 3 August, Tyrone's birthday. Bless the pilots, they'd decked out the plane in birthday bunting, but nobody felt like celebrating.

Heather landed just before us and then she went straight to the Royal Marsden in Sutton. Her condition deteriorated rapidly and although they stabilised her for a couple of days and there was talk of getting her home, she was too critically ill to move.

Never mind the K Club, forget the Open or the worst thing I had ever previously had to contend with – those situations were nothing compared to what I was facing now. The hardest thing I have ever done in my life is to sit down with my kids and tell them that their mother is going to die and they will never see her again.

Dr Steve had been advising me throughout Heather's illness and the one thing that I'd wondered about most was when and how I would tell the boys. He had always advised against it while Heather was in no imminent danger. The boys had been into the hospital previously a couple of times, but I didn't want them to see her with wires and tubes coming out of her. They didn't need to see her slipping in and out of consciousness with her mind not quite functioning.

The care team that come in and advise when a patient is going through their last days were very sympathetic but also very straightforward. Now, with a few days at the most left, was the time to tell the boys that their mother was going to heaven. They stressed the importance of me telling them that they were never going to see her again. There was no softly-softly approach, they said. I basically had to get the two of them beside me and tell them exactly what was going to happen.

I would not wish having to do that on my worst enemy. It was as horrible and difficult as it gets and I knew there was no easy way to approach it.

I sat Tyrone, who was eight, to my right and Conor, who was five, on the left. I told them exactly what I had been advised. They both broke down screaming. It was the worst thing I have ever had to do, but I had to do it.

This time, they both grasped that she was not coming home.

Heather died two days later, in the early hours of Sunday, 13 August 2006, in London's Royal Marsden Hospital. She was 39.

Heather was a wonderful and enormously supportive wife and mother and friend. Her courage and bravery throughout were unbelievable and an inspiration to us all.

All in all, we had done everything we could to try to help extend Heather's life as much as possible. Just before she got really bad we had a very sensible conversation, which I will not reveal, but we talked well. The vast majority was about the kids, and as for me she asked just one thing. 'I want you to play in the Ryder Cup,' she said.

The quote on her tombstone, borrowed from Dana Reeve, wife of Superman Christopher Reeve, sums up Heather perfectly. It reads, 'Don't be sad for what you've lost, smile for what you had.'

There was much reflection in the days and weeks and months after Heather passed away. I would be the first to say that I had been far from the perfect husband – far, far from it. Because of the selfish nature of my job, it was my way all the time – my way, my way, my way. That's something I still battle with to this day, but to be successful in our sport, or at least for me to be successful, then I can't see any other way. Heather put up with an awful lot from me.

But the more time goes on, the more you remember the good times and not the bad. She has a constant presence in the house through her pictures and we still talk about her often. She will never be forgotten.

The unbelievable thing about Heather was that she never felt sorry for herself, never once. I don't know how she did it. I just don't know how she could not wonder why she had to be the one. She had a lot of things going for her, two wonderful kids, a husband who could be an idiot – but sometimes was OK. And she had a nice lifestyle. At 39 it should have been a case of 'Why me?' Why did she have to be the one in 10,000 who fell to this type of cancer? She never said it and I doubt that she ever thought it.

For a long time after she passed away I was in complete melt-down and didn't know what was going on. I really struggled with why it had to be Heather, why her. I wished it had been me, not her. I really did. Out of the two parents, I am sure that the mother is better suited to bringing up children alone. She would have been a much stronger influence than me as a single father.

My world came tumbling down and I couldn't see the way ahead. I slipped into relationships I shouldn't have and I didn't know what to do. I just could not see the light. I don't know if my mind had gone, but I just could not make sense of anything.

Throughout all the difficult times, Chubby and Sarah were trying to do everything they possibly could behind the scenes to make it easier for me. Without them I would have been ten times the mess I was. It was the first time Chub had been through anything like this with any of his players, but he was always at the end of the phone and I let him know what was going on all the time. Sarah was another angel as she tried to help me piece together my fractured life.

I admit that I went completely off the rails for a while, but if there were things I shouldn't have done, I knew there were others that I definitely had to do. The most important was to change my perspective on being a father. I had to change, because it could no longer be Heather who was there for them. It had to be me. I had to be there for them, and now I believe my relationship with them has exponentially improved. I had to put in the effort that Heather had always put in and I took for granted.

It was tough for everybody connected to Heather, not least the boys. They'd occasionally come through in the middle of the night and jump in bed with me, but whatever was going through their heads, they slowly but surely came to realise that although life would never be the same, it did have to go on. Dr Steve had assured me how unbelievably resilient kids are and that they would cope. His own had been through the same and come out the other side.

I must say that Papplewick were unbelievably brilliant with both Tyrone and Conor at this difficult time. Headmaster Tom Bunbury and his staff went above and beyond the call of duty and both boys have some very fond memories of the school. I was also fortunate to have the housekeepers, Eddie and Alice, living at home in the staff quarters. They are a wonderful couple and were there all the time. The kids needed them and more importantly trusted them. It was tough, very tough, but we did what any family in our situation has to do. We coped the best we could. Sometimes it was bad; sometimes it was really bad; sometimes it was horrific; and sometimes it was OK.

The funeral was a difficult day back in Northern Ireland, because the place where we were married would now be Heather's final resting place. The way it's done at home is that you walk from the church to the graveyard behind the coffin, and that's what we did. There was a big media presence, but fortunately the police managed the scene very well and made sure there was no intrusion. Although my relationship with the sporting press has been good over the years, when it comes to the more personal side it's a different media. The other day I came across a picture of me and the two boys walking behind the hearse. It was hard, but they coped well. Conor burst out screaming in the church, and Tyrone held on as best he could, but we were all bad.

We had a wake afterwards at the Salmon Leap restaurant. A lot of golfers and their wives attended because Heather was always a popular figure. She was in the Tour Wives Association and whenever there was a Ryder Cup, she'd be behind the bar at the after party and she always enjoyed herself.

While we were having the service in Northern Ireland, those who could not be there because of the US PGA Championship in Chicago had their own little service outside the clubhouse on the first morning of the event. Tom Lehman gave a moving address and that touched me deeply. He would go on to have some very kind words for me when he saw me at the K Club during the Ryder Cup a few weeks later.

One of the people who suffered most through the loss of Heather was her mother. She is a very religious person and I found myself afterwards asking her the question why, why, why. She had no answer. Probably she was still wondering herself how it came to pass that she would lose her own mother and her daughter exactly six years apart to the day.

Once everything settled down, we returned to England because one of the main things that Heather had said to me before she died was that she wanted me to play in the Ryder Cup, even though she realised it might be taking place not long after her passing. She was really adamant.

I immersed myself in the process of trying to get in the team. I used it as an emotional barrier. I tried to be there as much as I could for the kids, but spent hours and hours with coach Ewen Murray up at Queenwood. I would hit hundreds of balls, working away at my game, blocking out as much as I could. It was what Heather wanted.

It was what she got, because captain Ian Woosnam picked me and I threw myself at it. I'm sure I did her proud there, not just the way I played, but the way I controlled myself. I hadn't been in denial, but I hadn't let it all out either – until it was all over.

I admit there were times when I struggled to deal with everything. That in itself brought a lot of media interest and it came at a time when I wasn't able to cope with it. My job has always been in the public eye, but after the K Club it seemed that everything I did was a matter of public interest. I did not have time to grieve and that was very hard to handle and it drove me even further into losing the plot.

The six months before and the six after were all played out in the public arena. There were lenses everywhere waiting for me to burst into tears or get hammered. I felt as if I was always being watched. It was tough enough having to deal with Heather having passed away, but the intense media interest made it even more difficult.

The whole world came crashing down. But I did know that I had to become a proper father. I don't know if it was something I hadn't been able to do before or I'd been too selfish to do before, but I definitely had not had enough quality time with them. I know I left too much to Heather – I'd always be out playing or practising – but that option was no longer there. So what would be the best for Tyrone and Conor, I wondered.

Eddie and Alice had done such a wonderful job while Heather was alive and getting me through that very difficult period, but I started to think more and more that there would be many positives about moving back home to Northern Ireland. My kids would then have my family around them. I will thank Eddie and Alice forever for the great job they did, but it's a little different having the boys looked after by the family. And it wasn't as if they were new to it, because we'd gone to Portrush on a regular basis and they'd loved it. So it didn't just come out of the blue. Now they are both part of a big family environment again.

I think Heather would be very pleased with the way the boys have turned out. They still have their 'pleases' and 'thank you's', which she hammered into them on a daily basis. For the most part, they are two really good kids and I hope that they will stay that way.

I've tried to become a good dad and I think I'm doing a pretty decent job. I don't know that I am, but I think I am. And I'm sure she'd be delighted to know that we'd gone full circle and returned to Northern Ireland. The boys are losing their posh English accents by the day and they don't go to private schools any more. It's just a steady, normal carry-on and they are loving it . . . and their golf.

I'm very lucky to have my sister Andrea and her husband Davy looking after them while I'm away, and I am also very lucky to have found in Alison a woman who is just as strong-minded and opinionated as Heather and gets on extremely well with the kids, as they do with her.

13

OPEN COUNTDOWN

The build-up to the 2011 Open was a long, sometimes successful and occasionally painful process. I have never found it easy to accept that no matter how hard you work, or how many thousands of balls you hit in practice, there is no guarantee certificate attached to your efforts. And mine had too often been in vain. But whenever I have felt like pursuing different channels of employment or throwing the clubs into the deepest pond, I have always gone back to the game, determined to get my reward. After all, golf is my job and, to be honest, I'm not sure what else I could do.

I made a conscious effort in the first part of 2011 to show an uncharacteristic amount of patience – no easy task, believe me. I had worked as hard and as often as always, but I was also consciously trying to wait for things to materialise rather than pushing for them to happen. This was all new territory for me.

It had been three years since my last win and in a period like that you do stop and wonder if it is ever going to end. My main driving force was my conviction that I still had the talent to win again. I was in no doubt about that. It was purely a question of letting it surface. So my practice was its usual relentless self and I just hoped that at some point it would turn into my day again.

Unfortunately, there was no immediate improvement, either on the course or in my demeanour off it. My golf was mediocre, to say the least, despite the hours I was putting in. Absolutely nothing was happening to suggest that I was emerging from that long barren spell and I was getting more and more fed up with the game.

After playing in Morocco at the beginning of April, I was scheduled to play in Malaysia before having a week off in the Bahamas to spend some time with the family. Chubby said, 'Forget Malaysia; you're not in the right frame of mind to play there. You need to get away, rest your head and have a holiday with your kids.'

That's exactly what I did. At this stage of my life, I had struck up a very strong relationship with Alison and she joined me in the Bahamas, along with the boys and Andrea, her husband Davy and their children Chris and Callum. I still mixed pleasure with some business, but although I practised really hard in Abaco, I managed to relax, went bonefishing and really enjoyed myself. I emptied my head, albeit for short a period, of any negative thoughts.

There were encouraging signs on the golf course too. In fact, I nearly won a competition. I played in the member-guest at Abaco with Davy, who was off 17 but should have been off about 27. We got to the final, but more important, I played quite nicely, so it was with renewed optimism and enthusiasm that I returned home for a day before setting off for Mallorca . . . and a tournament that would help shape the rest of my life.

* * *

Miguel Ángel Jiménez and me enjoying cigars during the 2004 Ryder Cup at Oakland Hills.

Tiger hug: before the 2006 Ryder Cup at Ireland's K Club.

Straight down the middle: my opening drive at the K Club at an emotional Ryder Cup.

Friendly face 1: Paul McGinley's wife Alison, Heather's close friend.

Friendly face 2: Phil Mickelson's wife Amy.

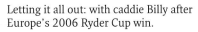

Letting it all out: with caddie Billy after Europe's 2006 Ryder Cup win.

Winning line-up: captain Ian Woosnam leads out his team for the K Club closing ceremony.

With fellow vice-captain Paul McGinley (*left*) and Padraig Harrington, Graeme McDowell and Rory McIlroy after the Celtic Manor Ryder Cup win in 2010.

Coach Andrew Simmonds looks on as John Duffy tees off, watched by Tom McKibbin, at my golf school in 2011.

Time to start the party: on the first tee at Royal St George's for the last round of the Open Championship in 2011.

Rough-going: digging deep on that unforgettable Sunday.

Just one good swing: preparing to drive for the final time as caddie John Mulrooney looks on.

Mum, Dad and Alison behind the 18th at Royal St George's.

...elebrating with co-author Martin ...ardy.

Jug of joy: sharing the moment with Chubby in the Royal St George's locker room.

Local hero: Andrea leads the cheers in the Bayview Hotel in Portballintrae.

Bringing home the bacon: Conor nurses the jug while Tyrone goes spotty.

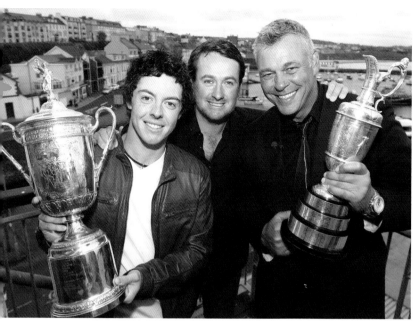

ster's finest: with US Open winners Rory McIlroy and Graeme McDowell.

hip off the old block: Tyrone drives off in the 2012 Irish Open Pro-Am at Royal
ortrush.

White wedding: with Alison at Abaco after our nuptials in April 2012.

Four behind at the start of the last round of the Iberdrola Open in Mallorca, I quickly ate into my ISM colleague Chris Wood's lead, but a double bogey on the 11th after finding water looked to have cost me the chance of a first win since the 2008 KLM Open. Chris encountered even more problems, however, needing 40 to come back, and could not claim a maiden victory. I holed out from the fringe on 14, hit an approach to six feet at the next for another birdie and had a couple of very good par saves before finally getting over the line.

It was a tough day for Chris and, although absolutely delighted at a win, I really felt for him. But I don't think the European Tour will have to worry about him, because I have absolutely no doubt at all that he will win.

The key to my win was patience and I'm sure if I'd remembered that throughout my career, I'd have had more wins to celebrate. It may have not been the biggest event or the best field, but after what I'd been through it certainly felt good. It felt even better because I had won on a very tough course. That season I'd wasted chances to win in Bahrain and Morocco, so to finally knock one off was special.

It was also extra special to have won in the homeland of Seve Ballesteros in the week that he had passed away. The European Tour would not be in the position it is today without him. He was the first man to do so many things and made so many breakthroughs. His cavalier style, flamboyancy and charisma attracted people to the game. He was a one-off. We would not have been there that week but for the Spanish genius.

I returned from Mallorca on easyJet – straight into Belfast from Palma. On the flight, I gave the stewardess my black American Express card and told her to buy everybody a drink. I think she was trying to wind me up by telling me the card had been declined.

So there we were. I'd won again and was in the kind of mood where I just wanted to win the following week and the week after and every week. It never works out like that, but by the time we arrived in Inverness for the Barclay's Scottish Open at the beginning of July, I was still playing well.

Pete Cowen had given me a new training aid designed to help with pressure and ball flight and I was hitting the ball very nicely for the pro-am and the first couple of rounds at Castle Stuart. But the weather turned ugly over the weekend and I quickly got demoralised.

That's been another of my problems. I can go from euphoric to suicidal in just a few holes. But in the coming week it would be the reverse. I would go from suicidal to euphoric in seventy-two holes. The realisation of the dream was in sight.

14

LAND OF OPEN GLORY

I had two options when leaving the northern highlands of Scotland. I could continue my journey to the lowlands of Kent or, which seemed by far the more attractive proposition, not bother. That was never going to happen, although it seemed pointless going to Sandwich when my head was all over the place and I was putting like a man with blurred vision. Yes, I had played well for the first couple of days at the Scottish Open, but I had got really frustrated on the final day and I was not on speaking terms with my putter when we left the course. It was not an uncommon situation.

I am not a golfer who can deal with humiliation or failure easily and I feared that would be my ultimate fate if I teed up in the oldest and greatest championship in the world. But neither do I believe in quitting, so deep down I knew I would complete the 630-mile journey south from Inverness rather than nipping back west across the Irish Sea.

Although I had my car with me in Scotland, my good friend Thomas Bjørn, not the best of flyers, offered to drive it all the way down to Sandwich for me – something that I was more than willing to accept, given that I felt far more like drinking than driving.

So I had a couple or three on the flight south, chatting away to American Ryder Cup player Matt Kuchar about the week ahead. He was looking forward to it. I wasn't.

There have been many low points in my professional life – feeling low being a common state of affairs among those searching for golf's unattainable perfection – but with my favourite event of the year just days away I was lower than a snail's backside.

Those at ISM who have had the fortune or misfortune – depending on my mood of the week – to look after my interests on the road jokingly refer to putting me on 'suicide watch' when I don't know where my next decent shot is coming from. They had therefore metaphorically changed my lace-ups for slip-ons, removed my tie and bolted the knife drawer when I arrived in Sandwich mid-evening on Sunday, 10 July 2011 . . . just three full days before Sandwich would become the centre of the golfing world's attention.

I wasn't looking for my game when I got there, just drinking partners. Finding the bottom of a bottle seemed a much easier and more enjoyable proposition than discovering where my ability to find the bottom of the hole had disappeared to.

There I was at the ISM hub house, where the week's food, drink and largesse would be dispensed in ever-increasing measures to players, employees, sponsors, press and assorted friends and guests. I was shaking my head and generally feeling as if my career was hurtling unstoppably into an unplayable lie . . . again.

There were plenty of familiar faces among the early arrivals. Chris Leigh, the house maître d' and ISM's travel and hospitality guru, was already in place, as was Chef Paul, who never leaves us hungry. I call them Dwarfy I and Dwarfy II respectively and affectionately, and hold them responsible for some of my girth. Dwarfy II's triple-cooked spicy chicken wings are unbelievable.

As the clock ticked that Sunday evening, however, the idea of hitting the hotspots of Sandwich or Deal, if indeed such animals existed, became less and less attractive. And if I was going to make a fool of myself a few days later, I didn't want anybody to be able to turn round and say it was because I had had a skinful on arriving in Kent.

Discretion won and we just had a few quiet beers. I was in bed far earlier than I had originally intended. The Open Championship, the one that dreams are made of, was just a few days away and deserved every respect. It was going to be my twentieth attempt at getting my hands on the silver claret jug, but I felt I had more chance of swimming the nearby English Channel to France in concrete flippers.

I was still very annoyed when I woke up on Monday morning, which had more to do with losing my golf game than the sore head I was nursing. The last place I wanted to go was the golf course, but my professionalism overruled my mood and I went up and did a little practice, which surprisingly didn't feel too bad. My overall feeling, however, was that I was still working towards something that would ultimately prove a waste of time.

Off the course, everything was fine. I was in a house with Lee, Chubby, Neill Hughes, a good friend and ISM director, and Selwyn Nathan, another long-time friend and recently appointed chief executive of the Sunshine Tour, while Philippa Woods, commonly called Posh because that's how she sounds, was our chef for the week and a good one at that.

Selwyn is always good at lightening the mood and he certainly did that with his pyjamas. Every morning he'd come down sporting a brand new pair of either Paul Smith or Ralph Lauren creations, which made everybody do a double take. If it was a bundle of fun at the house, now I had to find a way of enjoying myself once I got to the course. That would take more than a loud pair of pyjamas.

At one point Louis Martin, now with ISM, just told me to snap out of my mood and remember that ahead were four days of links golf, my favourite form of the game. I knew where Louis was coming from, but he couldn't know what I was going through mentally.

Coach Pete Cowen and ISM's Ian Garbutt, a former European Tour colleague and another one good at lifting spirits and saying positive things, had more of an idea, and knowing my preference for early practice, they were there on the range on Tuesday morning. But what Pete and Garby didn't appreciate when they spotted me with shoulders round about waist level and caddie John some distance behind was the strength of the verbal volley that would soon be heading in their direction, no matter how reassuring they were planning to be.

'Morning, Darren. All right?' said Pete.

'No I am ******* not,' was my reply.

'That good, is it?' said Pete.

'Horrendous, played like a **** Sunday – couldn't do anything. No control on my ball flight; no control of the spin; hitting way behind it; no pressure on the ball; and I can't ******* putt. Apart from that, everything's great.'

It was nothing that Pete hadn't heard tens of times before and I could see him saying to himself, 'Here we go again,' while looking round to see if there were any of his other pupils he could escape to. There were none to be found at such an early hour, so Pete was forced to stay and talk me down – something he is particularly adept at.

Pete's attempts to lift my spirits and reconnect me to my game included the words 'Don't forget: if there is a better bad-weather player in the world, then I haven't seen him . . . and the forecast is horrendous.'

Pete's thinking was that if he could get me with the same control on my ball flight as I had shown the previous Thursday and Friday in Scotland, then everything would be as it should be. He gave me simple thoughts about straightening my right arm, where to put my wrists and how to use my body. Within an hour I was hitting any shot they asked for.

'That's fantastic,' said Pete.

'Yes,' I replied, 'but I still can't ******* putt.'

I wasn't alone in feeling that this was not going to be my week. Oddsmakers were so impressed with my credentials that they found very few of the 156-strong field to place below me and I was on offer at 150-1.

At 42 years and 337 days, my age was against me. There had been only three older drinkers from the silver claret jug: Tom Morris, in 1867, aged 46 years and 99 days; Harry Vardon, in 1914, when winning the last of his six titles aged 44 years and 41 days; and Roberto de Vicenzo, the Argentine, who was 44 years and 93 days when he claimed the title in 1967.

Bookies, doubters, pundits and press agreed that my chances were between slim – one of my many nicknames and for the life of me I can't think why – and nil. Nobody suspected that I would be the main character in the annual chase for golf's Holy Grail just a few days later.

Or perhaps the R&A did.

I was surprised to find that they had given me a locker in the champions' section and I was next to Americans Justin Leonard and Tom Watson. I thought somebody had made a mistake. The locker I was using was the very same one that Greg Norman had occupied on his way to victory in 1986. I was told by an R&A member that when Greg had pulled out this year, they had wondered who they could put in there who would be quite unassuming, someone the champions wouldn't be bothered about and who wouldn't take offence. Somehow they'd come up with my name.

I texted Greg and told him, 'Thanks a million for pulling out because I got your locker.'

Would the bookies have been so generous with their odds had

they known that? Probably. Mr Watson, on the other hand, was more in the R&A way of thinking, because he told John, my caddie, that it might well be a lucky omen for us.

My mindset was not improving measurably, but I told myself to enjoy what I could. I'd left London after thirteen years the previous summer to return to Northern Ireland and I'd been practising on links ever since, quite a bit of the time in the kind of weather we could expect in Sandwich. I felt at home on links and in the weather. I was at the world's finest golfing event on terrain I was not only familiar with, but also comfortable on. Why shouldn't I enjoy it? There was no reason not to and it wasn't as if every aspect of my game wasn't functioning. If the putter started to behave, then things might just work out.

I teamed up with Lee Westwood for a few holes on Tuesday afternoon, but the putter was still serving solitary confinement in its compartment in the bag. It would not be released until the following day. Some wondered why I wasn't putting, but I didn't see the point, and in any case I had been on a reconnaissance trip to Royal St George's a couple of weeks earlier, when I'd done most of my homework about the greens.

The R&A had also done their homework, because they had factored in a new strip of semi-rough rather than going straight from fairway to long, which I'd always considered bordering on the unfair. That's one of the good things about the game's rulers. They look at what's happened in the past and use whatever they learn to provide a fair test.

* * *

If there was any consolation when I woke up on Wednesday it was that I was actually hitting the ball as I wanted and had control of its flight – always important, but even more so on links. Nevertheless, I wasn't in the best of humour when I teamed up with the newly crowned US Open champion, Rory McIlroy, for my final practice round in the morning. I was still only using the putter sparingly and reluctantly.

We're both pretty quick players and by the time we reached the 11th we were being held up by Louis Oosthuizen, who had triumphed at St Andrews the previous year, and his good friend Charl Schwartzel, who had donned the green jacket of Augusta just a few months earlier. I was in impressive company and Rory could not resist reminding me of the fact. We decided to join up, make it competitive and have a match. I may not have been putting well, but Rory was my partner, so I thought this was the perfect opportunity to nick a few quid off the South Africans. Sure enough, Rory birdied the first two holes.

Now, whether it was deliberate or by pure chance I don't know, but as we walked off the 13th tee, I was suddenly 20 yards ahead of the other three. It's not uncommon when my head isn't quite where it should be, so I may have orchestrated my own wind-up downfall, because suddenly Rory shouted out, 'Hey, Clarkey, where's your major?'

I may have been playing with three Grand Slam title holders, but my reply was both curt and rude. I was actually more worried about beating our opponents. Separating South Africans from their money is no easy task, particularly Charl, who, like royalty, doesn't do cash. Seriously, though, Louis and Charl are two of the nicest kids you could ever wish to meet and they handed over their £20 notes as soon as we'd finished. At least I had won something that week.

A posse of principally Irish journalists walked along with us for some holes and were waiting to grab a few quotes when we finished. It did not surprise or disappoint me in the least when most of their questions were about Rory and his predecessor as champion of America, Graeme McDowell. The pair of them deserved all the attention and credit coming their way and, after all, I hadn't given the scribes much to write about through my own recent endeavours.

15

GOING UNCONSCIOUS

I still wasn't totally at ease with the situation or my own demeanour, but the day before Ivor Robson, the R&A's official starter, was due to summon the world's best golfers to the tee, I was on a crowded practice green when I spotted a familiar face through the throng.

Dr Bob Rotella, golf's best-known sports psychologist, was there with his clients of the week. Just about every top golfer has been to him at some stage during their career and I had been a regular subscriber to his pension fund.

'Dr Bob! My saviour! Please give me some time,' I pleaded.

No is not in the good doc's vocabulary and very soon we were head to head and, more importantly, making headway.

I hadn't seen Dr Bob for quite some time, mainly because most of my golf had been played in Europe, but I knew that if anybody could help with my game and mentality it was the American author of *Golf is Not a Game of Perfect* and many other books. I was still concerned about my putting, that perennial problem for many golfers and one which drives some of us bonkers. If I feel that I'm putting well, my whole game seems to be better, and that's what I wanted to get sorted.

The Doc had a little time to spare and was more than happy to share it with me in the cold and drizzle. We made our way to the area reserved for members and chatted away merrily in between interruptions from autograph hunters and well-wishers. They all apologised for interrupting, but by that time they already had and I was happy to oblige them.

'See this, Doc,' I said. 'This is what I do. I'm lovely to everybody else, but I'm miserable to myself.'

I told him that since I'd won earlier in the season, I'd basically screwed up by trying to perfect my swing and putting, instead of freewheeling a bit. One guru had told me this, another that, but nothing worked. I let out all my feelings, explaining that I was being driven crazy by frustration and disappointment; the more I practised, the worse it got, but I still kept doing it. I just could not get out of the cycle that was strangling my ambition.

I wanted the Doc to get my putting and attitude squared away, because that would remove some of the pressure from my ball-striking and iron play. I told him I was in such a dire place that I was convinced I had to take on every pin with my approach shots and hit it to a foot at most, or I was never going to make a birdie. I was forcing all my pitch and bunker shots because I knew I had to hit them to an inch.

I told him that I had tried several different approaches, even in the middle of rounds, and although I wasn't too bad standing over three- and four-footers, I just wasn't making anything from six to fifteen feet. Actually, it had been six feet to anywhere longer, because my speed control was terrible and I could never find the middle of the putter face. It's not as if I was standing over putts, seeing them have a chance and then watching them miss at the last roll. They were missing as soon as they left the putter face.

Dr Bob reminded me that everything he'd ever read or heard suggested that I had been a really good putter when I was in my teenage years. 'You know how to putt, so stop pretending you don't,' he said. 'And you have to stop trying to do what someone else tells you is correct. You've got to putt like Darren Clarke putts, not how anybody else says you have to.'

He reminded me of the events where I'd managed to 'get out of my own way' and just putt by instinct. I had to remember that when I did that, the putts dropped. The Doc told me to stop trying to force the ball into the hole. I wanted so much to make things happen that I was trying to guide the stroke. 'You have to be like Tom Watson or Brad Faxon,' he said. 'See it and hit it and accept whatever it does. At the moment you're fighting a war with this thing . . . and you're not winning.'

The Doc's words came in a simple, steady flow. He reminded me that when we'd worked together before and I had putted satisfactorily, it was because I had been totally unconscious in my preparation and execution. I'd reacted unconsciously to the target. I used to love the idea of seeing the target and hitting the ball, but now it was scaring the hell out of me. There was nothing unconscious: I was thinking, changing my mind, doing everything but what used to come naturally.

It was a question of simply believing I could putt and then going into an unconscious state. I had to putt with my eyes and instinct, because when my conscious brain was removed from my body, I saw it and committed to it. I must not walk up to the ball until I had committed to the shot. But once I got to the ball, there was no more decision-making to be done, no more time to think.

I had to just set up over the ball, look at the target and hit the ball. I had to get rid of all the indecision, the little doubts, the second-guessing about the read, the worrying about speed and line. I had to look where I wanted the ball to go and then hit it.

The Doc took me back to some basic things we'd done in the past. He picked up a golf ball and we started to play catch. I would throw the ball to him and after he'd thrown it back, he'd move three feet forwards or back, to the right or left. He'd put his hand up and I'd hit it with my throw every time.

'It's amazing,' he said. 'No matter where I stand you hit my hand, but when you threw it, did you know where your weight was, did you aim your throwing arm?' Negative.

'So how did your hand aim if you didn't tell it?' he continued. 'You not only hit my hand, but threw the ball at just the right pace so that it didn't hurt when I caught it.'

I replied, 'I never thought about it.'

'The point is you unconsciously knew how to throw it to me without hurting. And that's what your putts will do if you stop worrying about them. If you worry about leaving it short, you will gun it, and if you worry about running it by the hole, you'll ease up on it. Just believe that if you looked and trusted, then it would go at the right speed and on the right line; you don't have to tell yourself *how* to do it.'

The penny was starting to drop. I just had to trust that I was as good at putting as I was at throwing a ball.

'You have to remember that the person who designs a putter is probably an engineer and they've designed the putter so it does what it's supposed to do,' he said. 'God gave us gravity, so the ball is always going to roll and we've got a round ball, so the ball is better than a wheel because it's round on all four sides, so to speak. It doesn't matter what side it rolls on, it's always going to roll end over end.

'It's like when we were sitting over there a minute ago. You were talking to me but signing autographs. Your autograph was legible but you were talking to me, so how do you sign your name if you weren't telling yourself how to sign your name? It's being and doing *unconscious*: you already know how to do it, so don't think you don't know how to putt.'

Doc said he came from a musical family. He'd played clarinet as a kid, his father saxophone and mother and brothers and sister the piano. 'I've been to many concerts and if you watch anybody playing the piano, they hear the music in their head and their hands are going 100 miles an hour, but they don't look at the keys. They always hit the right key – unless they think about it, and if they think about it and worry about which key to hit, then they mess up,' he said.

'That's just like putting. You have to see what you want, see your target, and your arms and hands and athleticism will take care of the ball going there at the right speed. But if you're *thinking* about it, not trusting it, then you're restricting yourself.

'Darren Clarke is a great athlete and a great golfer, so you've got to get back to being Darren Clarke. It's amazing, we're sitting here talking and when you talk you don't tell yourself what muscles in your mouth to use to make certain sounds or words. If I asked you how do you make the sound "w" and which muscles you use, you wouldn't know. Well, if it came out wrong and you started worrying about it, it could make you into somebody who stammers or stutters.'

The Doc said that twenty-five years ago he did a programme for the National Stuttering Association and had found that 98 per cent of stutterers could go into their own room and speak fluently, but once they were in public they were very self-conscious because of previous bad experiences of pressure being put on them as kids whenever they said anything that didn't come out as it should. The majority stuttered in social situations because of the anxiety involved, because they were afraid of looking bad, and so they thought about it before they talked. He told me about the great country singer Mel Tillis, who had little confidence when he spoke because he was worried about stuttering, but when he sang country he sang fluently. He was using the same muscles in his mouth but had a different perception.

I was having a different perception of my putting. When you think you're not a good putter, or never going to make a putt or never even going to get a break, then the by-products are doubt and fear. That has an impact on the conscious mind, which in turn totally interrupts the rhythm and flow of your stroke. Your brain doesn't know where the target is because you're more worried about your backstroke than where you want the ball to go. It was beginning to make sense.

The Doc then tried a different analogy. He asked if I'd driven to the course and if I'd made any calls along the way. I said I'd called Alison, the boys and my parents. He said wasn't it amazing that while driving my car I'd managed to talk on the telephone and not have any accidents. He bet that I'd never told myself to stay in the driving lane, that subconsciously I knew to miss the other cars and end up at the course. I'd told myself before I got in the car that I wanted to go there and that's what happened.

He said he remembered the last time he was at my house in London and we were kicking a football around with the boys in the garden and we all instinctively knew how far ahead of the boys to pass the ball and how hard to hit it. We hadn't told ourselves to do it; we did it instinctively.

'Fear is an illusion,' he said. 'It's like a mirage and the only place it exists is in your head. And if your head thinks it's real you can convince yourself of almost anything. Golf is a game and it has to be played at, and you have to play it as an athlete, and an athlete plays with an unconscious mind. I don't care if it's putting, ball-striking or basketball or soccer, you have to go unconscious.

'I could take you to any other game we play. Whether it was snooker or pool, you'd know what to do and you'd just do it. I promise you when you hit a cue ball you're looking at the side of the other ball where you want the cue ball to hit; you're not telling yourself what to do with your arm. So why would you do it in the sport you're the best at? Why would you think consciously? You have to go unconscious, because that's the way you've been when you've been the best.

'A lot of guys say to me it's scary to go unconscious. I say it's scary for everybody else too, and if you want to separate yourself from the others in the field you have to go more unconscious and let go, and when I say let go I mean letting go of conscious control. Conscious control is something you do when you're worried it's not going to go where you want it to go. If you knew it was going there, you wouldn't think.'

The Doc told me I also had to get back to being my own best friend on the golf course. 'The only relationship between trying your hardest and doing your best is that as long as you're trying your hardest, you're never going to be able to do your best,' he said. 'We want you to do your best, not try your hardest.'

At this point we were on the putting green and Doc told me a saying from American football coach Vince Lombardi. Among the legendary Green Bay Packers leader's quotes was 'Tiredness makes cowards of us all.' The Doc said I'd been working so hard on my game that by the time the tournament arrived, I was so exhausted that I didn't have enough energy to deal with whatever challenges the course threw up. I had to get back to trusting myself, trying less and relaxing more.

'When you worry it's like you never think you're ready, so you're trying to get ready, and by Thursday you're physically and mentally dead, never mind by Saturday and Sunday. You have to rest and be fresh. I want you to wake up tomorrow morning and be excited that the golf tournament is starting,' he said.

I loved the quote from Lombardi. The Doc told me that he had been the toughest guy in the world as a football coach. His father had drilled into him at an early age the two things he had tattooed on his hands. On one it said 'work hard' and the other said 'play hard'.

'For the last forty years, most football coaches don't play much golf because they don't want anyone to think they're screwing around or having fun,' he said. 'They sleep in their offices because then if they lose everybody knows they're working hard, but what no one seems to remember is Lombardi was a golf addict. They somehow don't want to remember that he played as often as he could.'

He told me that I had to be rested for the weekend so that I could deal with all the bad breaks and adversity. I asked how Padraig Harrington, another visitor to Doc Rotella's consultation room, managed to do it when he was famously even more analytical than I was.

Doc told me that Padraig asked a lot of questions and wanted to understand everything, but when he was on the golf course he was no longer thinking about how to do things; he was seeing his target and hitting it. He was playing unconscious, the way kids do when they start the game.

'I bet you when your kids go to play golf they're just going to play with Dad. They don't go out there and say, "I better break 90 or it isn't going to be worth doing this,"' he said. 'If you love golf you have to love golf unconditionally; you can't just love it if every bounce is a good one, every ball goes to target, every putt goes in the hole and every break goes your way.

'What you should be learning from watching your kids play is that they're just out there having a ball playing golf. You tell me how much fun they're having back in Northern Ireland and they're with their buddies and they're out playing golf and one is wearing a John Daly outfit and they're feeling good. That's how it should be, so don't put a constraint on *your* game. Decide you're going to have some fun putting and you're going to have some fun playing golf. You've got to think, "I'm having fun. This is where the party begins. This is where I get an edge."'

We then went putting and he asked me to casually hit putts without much concern whether I made it or missed them. Just casually go up to the ball, look where I want it to go and hit it – no mind-changing when standing over the ball. I asked him what routine he'd like me to follow and was surprised when he said none. He wanted me to do whatever preparation I needed to, but when I got to the ball, just look and, when my eyes came back to the ball, hit.

'I don't want you thinking about a routine,' he said. 'I want you looking at the target and letting it happen. I want you unconsciously reacting to what you've just looked at, and I don't want you taking time when you come back to the ball, because you might get distracted and think of something else. Keep your conscious brain switched off. See it and roll it and, trust me, your speed and line will take care of themselves.'

All of a sudden putts were coming out of the face, my speed was good and I was making plenty. Then he had me putting from five feet with the heel of the putter and then the toe and I was making five in a row. And then he turned the putter round and had me putting with the end of the toe and still they went in – showing me that there wasn't just one sweet spot on a putter, that I didn't have to hit what I thought was perfect every time; there was room for error.

Then I had to putt with a sand wedge from eight to ten feet and I made eight out of ten.

'When I give you a sand wedge, you don't have these huge expectations because it doesn't matter if you miss. Just think about how little effort you're putting into aiming the wedge,' he said.

Finally we went back to the putter and he asked me not to say anything for the next twenty putts; just do what we'd been talking about, do instinctively what I felt and let whatever happened happen. The putts dropped relatively regularly. My mind, as coach Cowen would say later, had been freed . . . along with my putter.

From suicide watch on Sunday to ready for anything on Wednesday. Pete had sorted me out on the range and Doc Rotella on the putting green. I was ready.

16

THE OPEN: DAY ONE

I'd spent a bit of time earlier in the year talking with Mike Finnigan, the CEO of i2i Sports, whose company is dedicated to helping people hit their objectives and maximise potential by understanding the psychological strategies that lead to success. We wrote down my goals for the season and they included sitting down at Christmas with a couple of wins under my belt and an invitation back to Augusta for the US Masters. To meet those objectives, I would now have to win the Open. Mike also sent me a few motivational messages during the week, with every one of them ending the same way – PTAFW – Prove Them All ******* Wrong. I'd be trying.

As well as a sound game and positive attitude, other elements have to be factored in at the Open, not least the weather. Looking at the forecast, it seemed that my half of the draw would get the best of what was coming our way, but you can never be too sure by the sea. I feel perfectly at home in a seaside environment and, to be honest, the worse the elements, the more it suits me. My skin is well weathered from the lashings it has received from the winds whipping in from the Irish Sea. There was definitely a lot of Portrush in the weather, although the similarity between the two courses was far less obvious.

Sandwich is not as scenically beautiful as Portrush, which almost touches the Giant's Causeway, and it has been described as everything between vicious and quirky. What I knew about Sandwich was that it was a very stern test, not least because of its fiercely undulating fairways and the subsequent demands they make on second shots. This year, it was not only in excellent condition, but had been set up very tough yet fair.

Royal St George's is one of those courses where if you lose your cool, your chances of success go with it. Me? Patient? The two are not usually said in the same breath, but once the drama began to unfold I remained remarkably cool. I am reluctant to add 'calm and collected', but I even embraced those strangers as well. In fact, I would receive many texts over the four days from friends and fellow pros commenting on my attitude. They had all seen the other side, the one that had earned me another of my many nicknames, the Prince of Darkness.

This was the 140th Open Championship – a major, for me the best, being played on the kind of turf that the game itself was started on. Why shouldn't I enjoy it? Odds of 150–1 indeed. We'll see about that. PTAFW.

The first and second rounds would be played alongside American Jonathan Byrd and Y.E. Yang, of Korea, who had shocked the golfing world by beating Tiger Woods in the US PGA Championship of 2009. I'd played quite a bit with both of them and it was a good pairing, although I must say there aren't many bad pairings for me.

I still didn't know what to expect from my game, but, for some strange reason, I was calmer than I can ever remember coming into an Open. I had very much a 'que sera sera' attitude approaching the first tee, because the future was definitely not mine to see at that point. I was so relaxed that I was able to have a bit of friendly banter with the crowd.

I was bending over doing some stretches when somebody whistled and I immediately said, 'I hope that was a lady.' The crowd laughed, I smiled and the guy whistled again. I thought I must be doing something wrong, but I knew then that I was going to enjoy myself.

The key to my opening 68 was my putting, and for someone who is his own worst critic, I was actually prompted to say that I'd played very nicely – quite an accolade from me to me. My ball-striking had been solid, I felt relatively in control and the two bogeys I made were the result of driving into fairway bunkers. Those hazards at Royal St George's are particularly penal.

What was interesting was that it quickly became obvious that Jonathan Byrd hadn't played much links golf, because as soon as his ball ran off a green or was close to it, he'd bring out his lob wedge, whereas in similar circumstances I'd have my putter or seven iron in my hands.

The longer I was out there, the more I came to realise just how lucky we had been with the draw, but I wasn't feeling too sorry for the guys who went out in the morning. Being trapped on the wrong side evens itself out over time. I'd been there often enough and I felt I was due a slice of good fortune.

I expected a lot of better scores in the afternoon and, while quietly satisfied with my opening 68, I was delighted that Thomas Bjørn led the way with a 65 at the scene of his worst hour in a major. It was wonderful that he was able to put everything behind him and produce such a good round on the first day.

He shared the opening-day honours with amateur Tom Lewis, who few knew before the start, but many would know by the end. We don't hear much about amateurs when we're on the Tour, unless they are like Rory, so everybody was keen to watch the progress of Tom, named after five-time Open champion Tom Watson.

I was now determined to enjoy the week and bring plenty of positives to a championship that had started on such a negative note. Two under was not a bad opening effort at all, and something not expected of a 150-1 outsider. It was a solid start and a firm foundation.

Back at the house there was an extremely relaxed atmosphere, even though we were invaded by the BBC's 5 live team as they presented *Freddie Flintoff's World of Sport*. Freddie's always good for a laugh, so we had no problems continuing the fun that had replaced earlier despair.

17

THE OPEN: DAY TWO

Sleep, as ever, came easily and I was up and out in good time to prepare for an early start. The Doc was still dispensing advice and I was all ears. I told him that the previous evening I had not been able to stop myself watching the day's highlights on television, because I wanted to see my putting stroke. I had felt a certain wristiness during the round, but when I watched the replay it hadn't looked that way at all.

'There's a big difference between what you're feeling and what you're doing,' he said. 'That's why I don't want you to worry about it, because you could get very screwed up.'

I told him that every putt had come off the middle of the putter face and they were all starting on line and the speed matched everything else.

'Why wouldn't it be so?' he said. 'You weren't amazed when you were throwing the ball to me and every time you hit the intended target.'

I told him that I *was* amazed how well I was doing and putting, because I was not trying to set up correctly or get the ball position perfect. I wasn't thinking about the aim and instinctively the speed was right. I could see the Doc saying to himself, 'My word, maybe he *was* listening when we spoke yesterday.'

The Doc asked me to hit five bunker shots and they all threatened the hole.

'Do you know how much you opened the face of your sand wedge?' he said. 'Do you ever think about the face, or do you ever think about how much to open up your stance? Do you ever think about how far to take it back and how hard to swing to make it go the right distance?'

I answered no to every question.

He said that most professional golfers never think about such things when they are hitting out of a bunker, but put them on a green and the conscious golfer takes over. 'You're thinking to yourself, "I've fought to make this, so I have to. I'm going to feel bad if I don't." You put pressure on yourself all the time and that pressure takes its toll,' he said.

'You need to have the same attitude when you putt as you did when you were in the bunker. Putt with your eyes and your instinct. Putt as if you've removed your brain from your body. See it and instinctively respond to what you see and it will look like a great routine.'

I laughed when the Doc said that when I'd gone to college it was not to become a physics major, so why was I now trying to turn myself into one? He had no idea how I knew how hard to hit the ball, but he did know that my talents were my hand-eye coordination and a tremendous feel for the game – and I should use them.

'You've got to cherish and embrace your gift,' he said. 'Stop treating it like it's a curse, because that will make you mad, disappointed and heartbroken. Take advantage of it, ride it and milk it. Your gift will take you to heaven if you let it but to hell if you don't. You've just got to stop trying to control everything.

'You have a gift for putting, a gift for golf, so stop acting like you're uncoordinated and you don't have a gift. Your eyes and your instincts are brilliant, so all you have to do is look at a small target and react naturally and instinctively. You don't have to stare at the target, just casually look at it and react.

'It's fun and that's what the game is all about. When you're having fun, it's easy to be unconscious. When you're unconscious, it's easy to be process-orientated – where you're just looking and doing. When you get serious, you get outcome-orientated and you turn on your conscious brain.

'When you step on the putting green, you can either choose to believe that you're a great athlete or you can turn into a serious, uptight nerd. If you follow the former, you will be fine, but if you are the latter, then you're going to turn on your conscious brain and you're going to interfere with yourself. Stop trying to turn golf into a job that you hate. Stop working at it and get back to playing the game that you tell me you love.'

The Doc told me to treat my putter as if it was a friend, because it actually did make it easier to roll the ball on the green. A guy with a putter was always going to be better than a guy using his hand to putt. What I was doing was treating it as if it was actually making things harder.

'Stop fighting the putter,' he said. 'You've got to love to putt because you have to build your golf game from the putting green back to the tee; you can't beat the game from the tee forward.'

It was with that in mind that I set off for the second round, and although the weather gods weren't exactly shining down on us, they were definitely less active than they would be for those who followed in the afternoon.

There may have been a sense of déjà vu with a second-round 68, but only the number was the same. It was much more of a mixed bag than first time around. The Friday round included good and not so good and a little adventure, where previously there had been a basic solidity and almost predictability to my game. Thankfully, I was still in control of what had previously been my worst enemy – myself. I was not getting in my own way.

I'd also pulled off one shot that I was especially proud of. A couple of mistakes on 14 and 16 were still niggling away at me when I faced a tough shot into the last green. I knew it would be a big bonus if I made birdie and the best way to achieve that was to cut in a seven iron.

It was either a very brave or a very stupid call – I frequently swing between the two – but I executed it as well as I could have hoped for. The ball did exactly what I wanted in the air and settled down some 20 feet behind the hole. I thought about nothing more than holing the putt, and that's exactly what happened. It was a sweet way to end the round.

So I was four under at halfway and some of the world's best players were already on their way home. I could afford a wry smile in another direction, too, because I noticed that the weather forecast for the weekend was far from good. That was something I could look forward to. Tough weather on an already tough course. What do they sing? When the going gets tough . . .

I also knew I had a fifteenth club in my bag. The crowd at Sandwich had been more than supportive. They were filled with a high-voltage enthusiasm, which I appreciated very much indeed. It had been a while since I'd heard such shouts and roars and they made for sweet music. The crowd only responds like that to good shots, so I told myself that I'd better keep hitting them otherwise things might turn quiet again.

For the second day in succession, I was not only high up the leader board, but also invited into the media centre after my round for interviews with the world's press. You can always count on a few curve balls, particularly from the English journalists, and one questioner delighted in asking me if I was as surprised as he that I was sitting on the podium. As usual, I gave back as good as I got and then we quickly moved on to a more serious line of questioning.

'Do you think you can win?' was asked in various forms. They were looking for a stupid answer from somebody who might not know any better, but at 42 I wasn't going to fall into that trap. Of course I thought I could win, but thinking and doing are two different things and we'd have to wait and see.

I assured my questioners that it was not possible for me to face a more daunting task in golf than the one I had on the Friday morning of the K Club Ryder Cup. The Open was massive, the biggest championship in the world – it was something I had wanted to win since I was a kid – but it was not likely to throw at me anything that would induce the range of emotions I went through on that first day just outside Dublin. I would not face anything that would provoke more trepidation. That was the hardest thing I had ever done in golf, so what was there to fear about a weekend in contention at the Open?

I was asked if my return to the mix in 2011 after a couple of lean years could be put down to anything specific and I was able to explain that a much more stable home life had made it easier for me to focus and play better. Foremost in that was the return to Portrush from London. The move was predominantly for the sake of the boys, but it had also been beneficial to my golf, particularly of the links variety. The weather isn't always that bad in Portrush, but practising had definitely been easier in London. So during the winter of 2010–11 I'd had to get used to playing in less favourable conditions. Little had I known just how much that would help me six months down the line.

I was asked again about Graeme McDowell and Rory McIlroy. It had been suggested that I was jealous of what these two other sons of Ulster had achieved, but nothing could have been further from the truth. I was extremely proud of their back-to-back wins in the US Open and the help I had given them along the way, particularly Rory, who I had known from his early teens through my foundation.

I'd also thought it important to be part of Rory's victorious homecoming celebrations rather than travel to Germany for the BMW International. I was due to fly out on Monday morning, but having been so proud watching Rory, I felt Northern Ireland was where I should be. I called Marco Kaussler, Herr Golf BMW, and told him why I was withdrawing and he was very understanding.

Rory and G-Mac's successes had made no difference to me personally or the way I approached the game. Having two US Open champions in succession from such a small country was an incredible achievement and they were two excellent ambassadors. I was simply proud to come from the same place and that I may have given them a little help along the way. I hadn't known G-Mac as closely, because he had spent four years in America, but I'd played often enough with the pair of them and advised them on what they should and shouldn't do and what to expect when they turned pro. It seemed to have been good advice.

When all the scores were counted, quite late on Friday evening, the leader board showed that I was sharing the lead with American Lucas Glover on 136, with Thomas one shot back, alongside Spain's Miguel Angel Jiménez, Germany's Martin Kaymer and American Chad Campbell.

The hub house was its normal busy self, populated by an eclectic mix of ISM players and staff and other assorted invitees. The chefs there know each player's likes and dislikes and accommodate us perfectly, although there was one occasion when Chubby tucked into something that, unbeknown to him, contained tomato. He suffers an allergic reaction of quite monstrous proportions when he eats tomato, but fortunately he was able to control it before it got too bad – while reminding all concerned what the consequences of a repeat mistake would be.

There would be no mistakes that night as we tucked into curries, Chinese and even fish and chips – and everybody was appreciative of the efforts made to keep us happy.

I was in no way getting ahead of myself as I slipped beneath the covers on Friday night, but I was definitely looking forward to the weekend's activities.

18

THE OPEN: DAY THREE

My demeanour and mood from Wednesday onwards had become a topic of interest for many and it was something I touched on with the good doctor in the build-up to the third round.

Doc Rotella urged me again not to try too hard. 'You're really good at trying hard, but this week you've got to try less,' he said. 'You have to get past the fear and guilt that makes you feel like you're not trying. You've done all the work, you know how to do it, just let it happen.'

He impressed on me that the mind controls the ball, not the other way round. 'When you get in trouble you play as if the ball owns your brain; that's not the way it works,' he said. 'The only way you're going to own the ball is if you own your mind. And don't forget, there's a really important connection between having fun, being relaxed, being process-orientated and being unconscious. There's also a very strong relationship between being serious, being outcome-orientated, being judgemental and having your conscious brain turned on.'

As ever, it took time to get through, but I was listening.

Being on the right side of the draw in any tournament is advantageous, but in the Open it can make a much bigger difference than normal. I definitely had the best of the conditions for the first two rounds and set out for my third round on the Saturday afternoon alongside former US Open champion Lucas Glover determined to make the most of my luck.

I was hitting the ball really nicely and was genuinely excited about playing, which had not been a common feeling too often in the previous couple of years. It had been solid and reasonably unspectacular golf so far – the odd long bomb and the occasional lucky bounce – but it had been good enough to get me in a position I hadn't been in at the Open for far too long.

Playing with Lucas on Saturday was also a bonus, because I'd got on well with him because of the Harmon connection. While I was seeing Butch, he was often with Butch's brother Dick, now sadly deceased. Lucas is very laid-back and we chatted about all sorts of things on the way round. I could not have asked for a better draw. Just like former Open winner David Duval, another good friend, there is much more to Lucas than meets the eye and it was fantastic to play with him.

I had one of the best ball-striking rounds I've ever had – the best I could have played – and I didn't let myself get despondent when I missed putt after putt. I just tried to stay patient and fortunately I did. If anybody had offered a 69 before I went out to play, I would have bitten their hand off. We played in terrible conditions for the first few holes and then it improved to such an extent that it was safe to say that Michael Fish was on my side again.

I'd expected somebody or even several to emerge from the pack and make it a crowded leader board, but that's not how it panned out. So I had a big smile on my face when we shook hands afterwards and Lucas just said, 'That was fantastic, great. Good luck tomorrow.' I knew I'd still need it.

The leader board now showed that I was out on my own at the head of the field, although I would have preferred a much greater distance between me and the chasing pack than just the one shot I would be taking with me into the final round.

When I was escorted into the media centre I was offering no prizes for guessing what line of attack would come from the scribes. After all, I had tried on nineteen previous occasions to lift the silver claret jug and had dropped it every time.

It was exciting to lead with just one round left, but I also had to be realistic. They would be the longest eighteen holes of my career and I was still a long way from the finishing post.

I was asked if deep down I'd stopped believing that one day I might be in a position to make it happen, and my inquisitor seemed surprised when I said no. Did I ever doubt I would get myself back in this position? No. Did I know it was going to happen? No. Did I hope it was going to happen? Yes. But did I ever doubt? No.

I'd been able to draw on all my experience of failure and success, and I had also remembered what former Ryder Cup player and now BBC commentator Ken Brown had said to me before my first Ryder Cup in Valderrama in 1997: 'Don't let your golf game determine your attitude; let your attitude determine your golf game.'

It was sound advice. My career has shown that when my attitude has been good, so has my game. I'd had a very good attitude since Wednesday and it had shown through in the way I'd struck the ball.

Now I had to take that into the last round. It would be a journey I would not take alone. I cannot say too much about the role the crowd continued to play. All week it was incredible. Even when I was grazing the hole or missing opportunities, they were still behind me. There's nowhere else outside Ireland where I would have got that kind of support. And among that cheering throng were my parents, Godfrey and Hetty, who watched every shot from outside the ropes. My fiancée, Alison, was also there, but not Tyrone and Conor – their own round at Royal Portrush deemed far more important than coming to Sandwich to watch Dad. Even if they hadn't been playing themselves, they'd probably have opted to sit in front of the television and watch.

It was definitely a case of so far, so good, even though my patience had been severely tested on the greens. There have been occasions when I have not been able to cope, but my feeling here was that I could do no better than my best . . . and that's what I was prepared to give. I hit some good ones, some bad ones, had a few good and bad reads, but over every one I tried my best. The time I had spent with Dr Bob had not been wasted. He'd got into my head and had me in the right frame of mind.

Some people seemed to think I'd have trouble coping with the vast amount of time there would be between the finish of my third round and the start of the last. Whoever thought that did not know me. I have absolutely no trouble killing time and what lay ahead would not be occupying too many of my thoughts.

I had a quiet Saturday night and a lovely meal with Alison and my mum and dad at the hub house. I fielded quite a few texts – most memorably from Tiger and also Rory. I'd spoken to Rory at Chubby's house earlier, but later he sent me a text basically repeating what I'd sent to him when he was going out to play at Congressional during his history-making US Open win. He was telling me to be patient, to keep playing how I was. Instead of me being the old wise one, he was trying to give me all the advice, and that made me smile.

Ewen also had a few words and all the support was greatly appreciated. Tiger's texts were particularly helpful, but I respect and enjoy our friendship too much to divulge what they said. Let's just say he was very encouraging.

It wasn't much after 9.30 and a very nice glass of red that my wife-to-be and I retired to Chubby's house . . . along with another woman who was with me all week. It didn't matter if I was in the lounge, dining room, bedroom or shower, Adele was always there – her fantastic voice booming out of my Jambox, Bluetoothed to the iPhone. I love music and my taste is Adele to ZZ Top, but the one person I wanted to listen to all week was Adele.

I'd been sleeping well, and even on a night when I could have been forgiven for having a few things churning over in my mind, I was comatose very soon after my head hit the pillow.

19

THE OPEN: DAY FOUR

I woke at eight, looked out of the window and noticed it was blowing a bit, which brought a smile to my face. Then I rolled over and had another couple of hours before getting up to prepare for whatever awaited me. I was ready for anything that fate might throw my way.

When I arrived at the course, I was in a very relaxed mood, much to the delight of Dr Bob. He had been wondering about what frame of mind I might be in. He need not have worried – initially anyway, because I would throw him a curve ball just before tee-off. But when he first spotted me by the entrance to the putting green, I had a huge grin on my face, was happily signing autographs and high-fiving all and sundry.

It was déjà vu for the Doc, because his mind went back to when Padraig Harrington won at Royal Birkdale. He'd got there half an hour before the off to find Padraig smiling and laughing and signing autographs. He was in a great mood and looked as if he had all the time in the world, when it would have been very easy not to talk to anybody and just turn inwards. And Padraig went on to win. Was my mood an omen?

The Doc greeted me with, 'Buddy, it's party time; one last time here today.'

I told him I was feeling great and not so edgy that I wasn't in control of my emotions. I said I had been nervous on the first six holes the day before because the reception I'd received on the first tee was so loud and warm it caused me to get a little conscious. Consequently, I'd become tentative and cautious with my putting. I had been concerned about running putts too far by, and that led to me leaving them short.

'You get conscious and careful and get in your own way,' he said. 'You have to be more accepting and not get mad or upset,' he added. 'Don't beat yourself up if something doesn't go right; just back off and laugh at yourself.

'Make your attitude more important than the outcome and keep smiling. You were doing a great job yesterday, looking at the gallery and smiling, and that helps you stay unconscious. Just enjoy the moment, because you've been waiting for it your whole sporting life.

'Remember, you only control you, so let's win the battle with yourself and you will be happy after the round if you do that. Let's forget about scoreboards, let's forget about others. Just love being in your own little world, chatting with your playing partner Dustin Johnson and your caddie and his caddie, and just have a ball. It's a party with other guys who love golf.'

If the doctor was worried about me staying on track, then what I said to him next certainly took him aback, even though he was quick at disguising it. We were just ten minutes away from the most important tee time of my life and for the first occasion since we'd started our chats on Wednesday, I slipped into a dark mood.

'I've been through some serious times in my life,' I said. 'Losing Heather, being by myself, bringing up the boys and other stuff. It's been tough and you start to wonder if anything good will ever happen. I could really use a break, Doc,' I added.

The Doc wouldn't be where he is today if he couldn't think on his feet and he quickly snapped me out of the negative and into the positive.

'The tough times you've been through, they're behind you,' he said. 'You have to believe that you're destined to have something really good happen to you, but you have to stay out of your way to let this happen. Believe me, some really good things will happen to you over the next few years. You just have to accept it. You're being yourself when you're happy and chatty and unconscious. Just keep doing what you're doing. And don't forget how good your touch is when you are unconscious.

'This guy here who is happy and loose and free and owns the world, that's Darren Clarke. You're unstoppable if you're unflappable, so you can't let anything faze you when you're out there. You can't let anything bother you. Be in a great frame of mind and mood and let nothing that happens out there change that. Just let it happen.

'I want you to play golf as if God had turned up in my room last night and said, "Hey Doc, you're going to spend some time with Darren Clarke this week and, man, have I got some good news for you. I'm God and I wrote the book on life. Darren Clarke is going to win the Open this week and there isn't a thing he can do about it. It's a done deal, so tell him he doesn't have to try. It's already done."

'In other words, Darren, I want you to play as if you were destined to win this tournament. If you knew you were going to win, you'd be laughing when you made a mistake, because it doesn't matter. You know how easy it is to play the game when you're feeling that way.

'You're telling me how you're in love with Alison and you're going to marry her and she loves your kids and your parents and how wonderful it feels. You have this great picture in your head, because now you can see the light at the end of a tunnel it's been tough to get out of. Now you have to have that same picture when it comes to your golf game.'

I told the Doc about the texts I'd received from Tiger, what they'd meant to me and how similar they had been to many of the things we'd been talking about. It meant an enormous amount to have Tiger's support and now I had to put what everybody had told me into practice.

I reminded myself that when I'd won the two WGC events and other big tournaments, I'd always been relaxed and calm – something I had not been able to do often enough. But today had to be one of those days.

It really was party time.

I was about to walk to the first tee and I was a little nervous – if I hadn't been, then something would have been wrong. I said to the Doc, 'If I go out there and have fun and enjoy myself and commit to every shot, I will have won no matter what the final result is, so that's my goal.'

It would have been easy to think, 'I'm 42, so this could be my last chance.' But that wasn't my thinking at all. It was simply, 'Do the best you can.'

As Dustin stepped on to the tee he was greeted as Open crowds greet all visitors, with enthusiasm and respect. He had plenty of support. Then the cheers started for me as I approached the most important round of my life. The roar was as loud as I'd heard anywhere outside the K Club during Ryder Cup week. They were 100 per cent behind me.

I have been in a very fortunate position throughout my career that spectators have warmed to me. Perhaps it's because of my personality and the fact that I like a pint. I'm just an ordinary sort of guy and I try not to have too many airs and graces. The crowd were certainly a huge factor on that final day.

I've known the starter, Ivor Robson, for many years and he's a wonderful man, and it seemed that even he was nervous for me. But there was nothing anybody could do now but wait and see. It was time to start the party. I shook hands with Dustin. I'd played with him before and knew he'd come close a couple of times in majors, so I was sure he'd be feeling exactly what I was inside.

These days it's almost as if you have to serve your apprenticeship in contention at the majors before you get a chance to win one. Very few claim their first without having been there before. Then again, quite some time had elapsed since I'd been there before, and an awful lot of things had happened. Yet you never quite forget the adrenalin rush. I've always said that, as a golfer, if you don't want to put yourself in a position where it hurts if you mess up, then it's time to stop playing. I was now facing the ultimate test.

So there I was on the first tee, having played 205 shots to get into the lead by one from my playing partner Dustin Johnson, with Rickie Fowler and Thomas Bjørn two shots further back. I was the only person from Britain and Ireland in the top sixteen at the start of play and there were no fewer than ten Americans all wanting to deny me my finest four-and-a-bit hours.

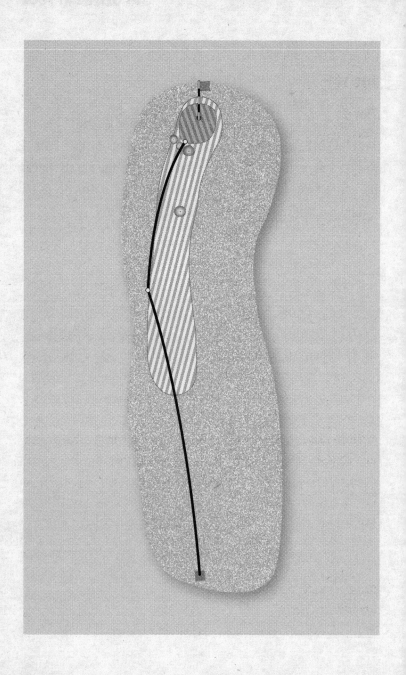

HOLE 1

Par 4
444 yards

For me, the defining holes of the round were not at the end, surprisingly, but at the start. They say a major doesn't begin until the back nine on Sunday afternoon, but it was on the first few holes that the platform for my success would be built.

On the first, the wind was off the right and I took a driver, pulling it left. I tried to hold up a seven iron for my approach, but it went to the back of the green. It was in a smelly position and not only was the breeze now coming harder, but the hole was cut in a little trough. When I hit my first putt, I thought it was perfect, but it pulled up ten feet short. On closer inspection it became apparent that one more foot of roll and it would have filtered down to the hole, so it had not been as bad as I first thought.

I didn't need a wake-up call to let me know what I faced, but I'd definitely had one there. A ten-footer to save par on the first is not what is required to settle you down when holding the slenderest of leads. Dustin had a five-footer for par, but it was me to go first and it looked a horrible task to avoid starting with a bogey. I just composed myself, told myself the outcome was irrelevant and calmly rolled it in. My partner missed his, so a difficult situation had suddenly turned in my favour.

Score on hole: Par
Standing to par: -5

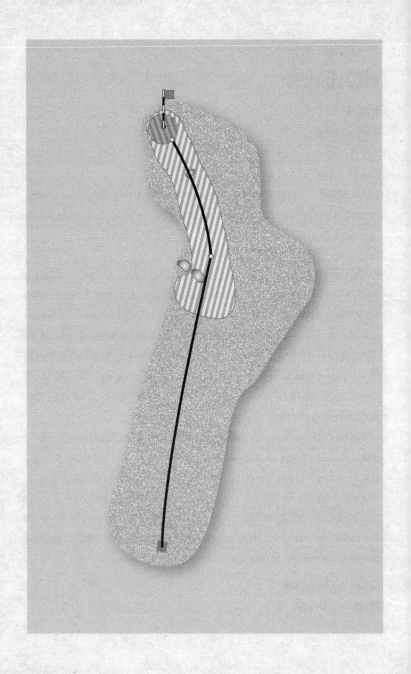

HOLE 2

Par 4
417 yards

On the second hole I hit a good tee shot and was then faced with something I'd been working on with Pete and Ewen – cutting a sand wedge against a right-to-left breeze to ensure the ball didn't spin away from the hole when the flag was on the right.

The shot felt perfect when I hit it and, as the wind howled in, I thought it would turn out the best I'd hit all week. The ball took one bounce and stopped without spinning just five feet or so from the hole and I knocked that in.

If putts can settle nerves, I'd holed two of them in succession.

Score on hole: Birdie
Standing to par: -6

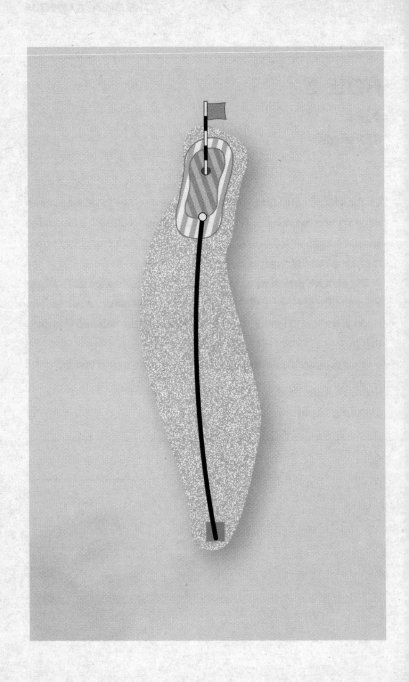

HOLE 3

Par 3
240 yards

I had another decent tee shot on the third hole, but it came up a little short and on the wrong level of the green. I putted up and over a ridge, but misjudged the pace and it rolled ten feet past, leaving me with another character-builder. But I was still intent on relaxing and letting the ball go to the target, and that's exactly what happened with my second putt.

Suddenly, with Dustin having made the odd mistake, I was three shots clear. Thankfully – it's a golfing cliché, but it's the truth – I managed to stay in the present. Not once, until I was on the 17th with a healthy lead, did I ever think about the possible outcome. How on earth I managed to do that, I don't know, but I did.

Score on hole: Par
Standing to par: -6

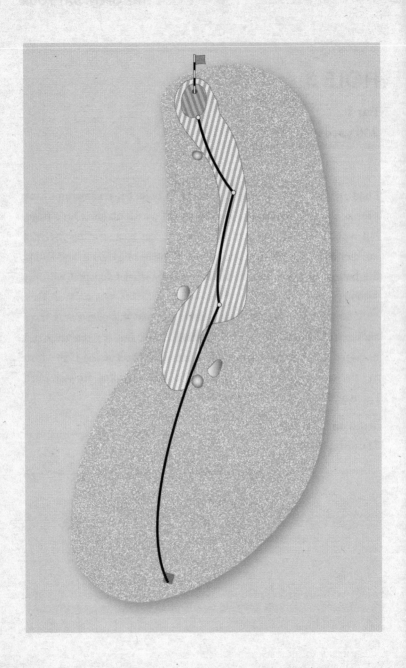

HOLE 4

Par 4
495 yards

On the fourth hole I cut a driver into the breeze, although I'd meant to turn it, and left myself a downhill lie with not much of an approach. From that I came up short, but then hit a good chip to eight feet. I missed the putt, yet instead of being cross I just said to myself, 'Fine, whatever.'

There have been plenty of occasions when that would not have been the case. I would have let the mistake fester and it would have affected my play for a few more holes. I was determined that that would not be the case on this day of all days. Calmness would be the key.

Score on hole: Bogey
Standing to par: -5

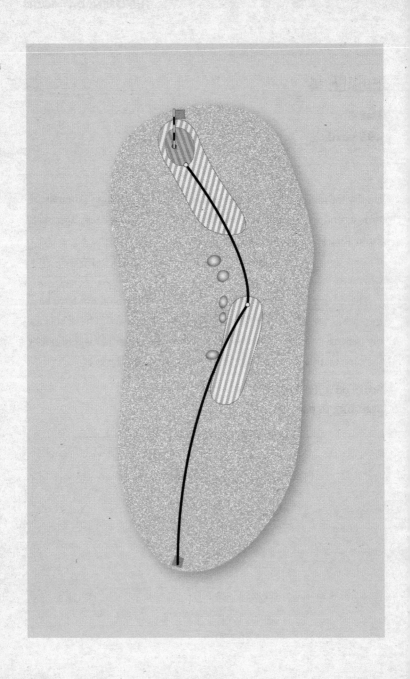

HOLE 5

Par 4
419 yards

The driver had earned pride of place in the bag and would continue to obey orders here - my tee shot leaving just 105 yards to go. The sand wedge wasn't quite as obedient and I was still 30 feet away when I reached the green. Two putts were all I needed and that was another bullet dodged.

Score on hole: Par
Standing to par: -5

HOLE 6

Par 3
178 yards

The first threat to my lead would come from a familiar figure, although one who had not enjoyed much success at the Open. My good friend Phil Mickelson was making a charge and I knew just how much he would enjoy putting me under pressure.

I was hitting the ball well, however, and for the most part my putter was behaving. On the sixth hole, I gave it a chance to excel when I hit a beautiful cut four iron against the breeze to 20 feet.

I was comfortable over the birdie putt and it looked good all the way – until the last second, when it decided it would need more help to find the hole.

Score on hole: Par
Standing to par: -5

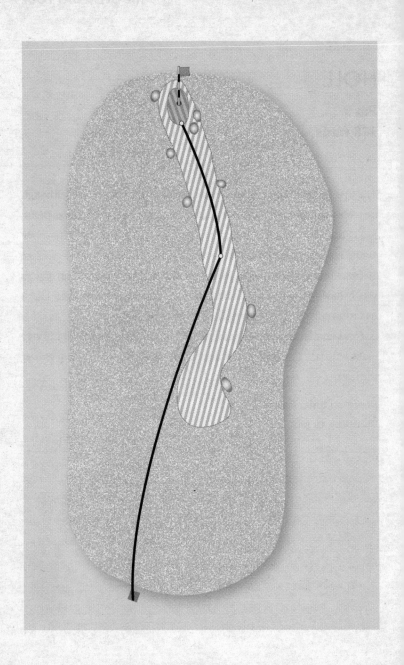

HOLE 7

Par 5
564 yards

At the seventh hole, although I pushed a solid driver a tad, it was OK and left me looking at a fairly safe seven iron. I was standing with my caddie John Mulrooney deciding what to do and I could hear roars, but didn't know who was doing what, so I just concentrated on what I could do. John told me it was an eight iron and it came out beautifully, finishing 15 feet from the hole.

As we were walking towards the green I spotted a scoreboard and for the first time Phil's name was up there as well. It was weird and I can't really explain it, but when I saw the scores, nothing really registered with me. It didn't mean anything. I had no idea what score he'd started at and it didn't make any difference to what I was doing. It transpired that Phil had been five shots back, but he picked all of them up in the first seven holes – his eagle on the seventh putting him alongside me at the top of the leader board.

I told myself just to concentrate on what was in front of me. The rain was now coming in, but it didn't stop my eagle putt catching the edge of the hole and dropping. Whatever company I'd had was now two shots behind.

Score on hole: Eagle
Standing to par: -7

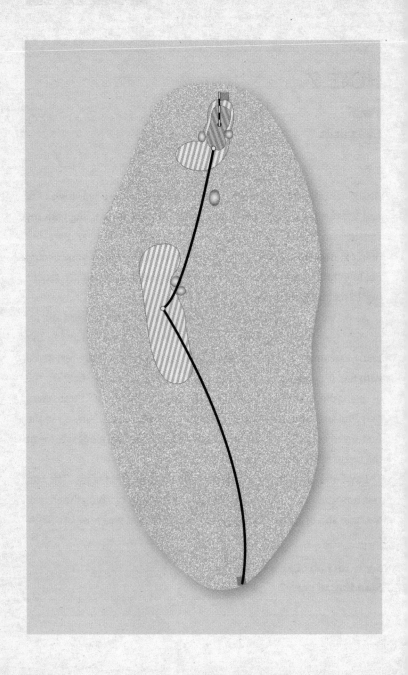

HOLE 8

Par 4
453 yards

The thing about Royal St George's is that there is no let-up, no chance for a breather. If you can take stock anywhere, it's definitely not on the eighth, where a par is more than welcome.

A nice enough drive left me with a five iron in and I finished it off with a couple of putts, which ensured no damage was done. What others were up to, I had no interest in.

Score on hole: Par
Standing to par: -7

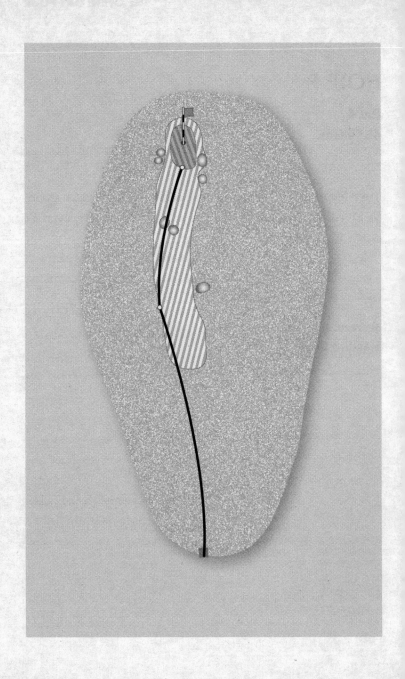

HOLE 9

Par 4
412 yards

Every champion gets lucky somewhere along the line and on the ninth hole I had a particularly fortuitous break that on another day may well have proved my undoing.

I'd hit a three wood there all week and this time I pulled it a little on to what I knew would be a downhill lie. I didn't think it would be anything that I couldn't cope with – until I got to the ball and found it in a horrible lie on a very severe down slope. I couldn't do much other than chip it out, so I took an eight iron and got steep enough on it to get it up into the air.

It didn't work out that way, even though I hit it reasonably well. The ball was heading straight for a bunker, but instead of hitting the face, it took one bounce, kissed an upslope and then hopped straight over and continued running up to the green. I knew I'd got away with one there, because missing the bunker meant I could make four, whereas I would have been staring at six or seven if I'd gone in. I was very happy to leave the green with a par.

Unbeknown to me, my lead was down to one again when Phil picked up another birdie on ten, but a missed par putt from two feet on the 11th started a decline that brought him four bogeys in six holes and the end of his challenge.

Score on hole: Par
Standing to par: -7

HOLE 10

Par 4
415 yards

The start of the back nine, the business end of any championship, and I'd reached that point without any damage to my prospects. In fact, I'd enhanced then, but there was still more than two hours of intense action and concentration ahead. Keep it up, keep going, keep calm.

Another decent drive left just 126 yards to go and a pitching wedge successfully negotiated them, setting up a possible and priceless birdie opportunity. I felt confident over the putt and it looked good all the way to the last couple of inches, when it decided it needed another tap to reach the bottom of the cup.

Score on hole: Par
Standing to par: -7

HOLE 11

Par 3
243 yards

The 11th stands comparison with any of the long short holes in the world in terms of difficulty. I chose a four iron and was perfect for yardage, unfortunately not for accuracy. It wasn't the easiest of bunker shots, but I was hoping for at least a little less distance than the seven feet I faced to save par. It was with relief that I exhaled as the ball disappeared.

Score on hole: Par
Standing to par: -7

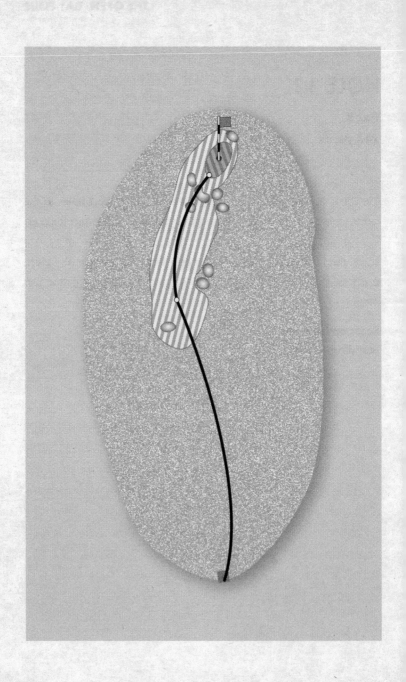

HOLE 12

Par 4
381 yards

I was very happy with my composure and ball-striking so far and the finishing line was getting ever nearer, although not quite fast enough for my liking.

Accuracy is paramount on this short par four and I found it off the tee and again with a 160-yard approach using a nine iron. Two putts meant another par on the card and another tricky hole negotiated.

Score on hole: Par
Standing to par: -7

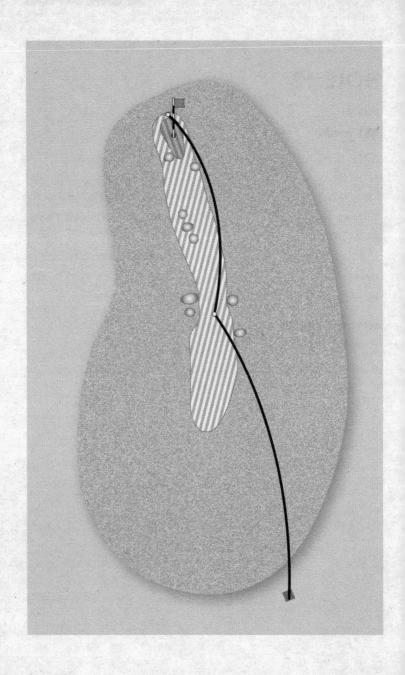

HOLE 13

Par 4
459 yards

The last six holes of the Open and here I was at the head of the field and whatever nerves I had been expecting had not materialised. I'd be more than happy if it stayed that way.

I had a nice drive on the 13th which left 169 yards and I felt sure an eight iron would put me in position for another birdie opportunity. However, the ball released far more than I anticipated and over the back of the green it went. Fortunately, there was so little trouble there that I was able to use the putter.

I would have settled for anything inside six feet, so I was not disappointed when I had four feet left for par – the kind of distance that commentators often refer to as a nerve-tester. Mine were shown to be steady.

Score on hole: Par
Standing to par: -7

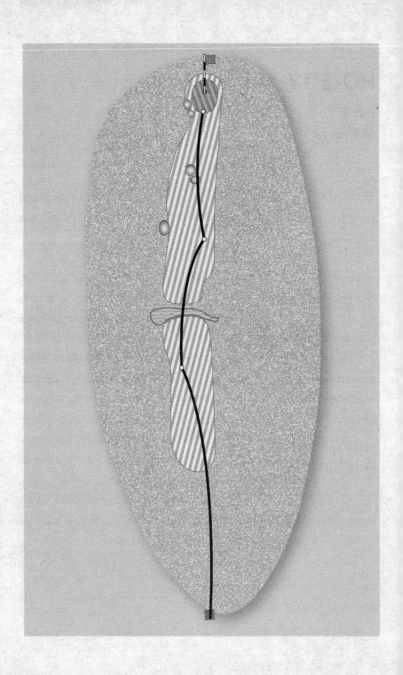

HOLE 14

Par 5
547 yards

Somebody was always going to make another charge and, sure enough, by now Dustin had started to give me a run for the winner's cheque. A couple of birdies had bitten into my lead, but then we got to the 14th hole and he came unstuck without my knowing.

This par five can be one of the most treacherous holes on the course and Dustin had the honour – flushing it down the middle as he normally does, an absolutely pure shot. I deliberately teed the ball low and punched a driver down the left to keep it safely away from the out-of-bounds on the right. I couldn't get there in two and John gave me a perfect yardage for a lay-up. I was in good shape and well away from anything that could do me harm.

I was thinking about my third shot when I looked back to see Dustin dropping another ball. I was trying to work out why he was doing that, as I hadn't seen him hit his second – and then I suddenly realised he must have hit it out of bounds. He had, but that wasn't going to change my approach. I told myself to hit my third shot into the middle of the green and forget about anything else. That's what I did, a lovely punched knock-down shot, followed by two putts for a par.

The danger hole was over, but not the Open.

Score on hole: Par
Standing to par: -7

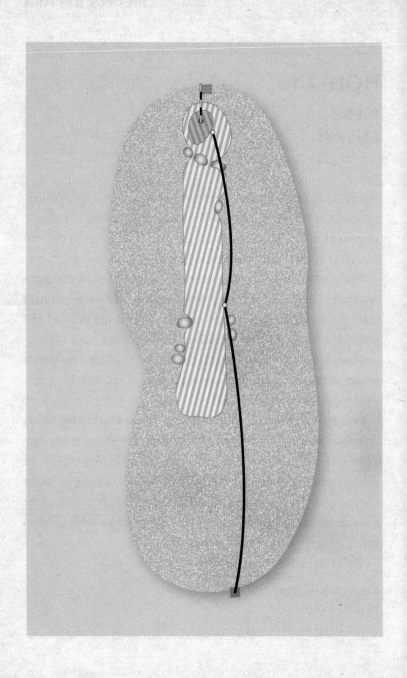

HOLE 15

Par 4
496 yards

On the 15th tee my mind strayed a bit because I remembered Billy Foster telling me about what happened when he was caddying for Thomas Bjørn and he'd had a similar lead to mine in 2003. Thomas had gone into the left-hand trap on the 15th hole and made bogey, so I aimed further right, hoping for a draw which I didn't get. I ended up in the right-hand rough in a terrible lie, but I'd figured out this hole in practice and decided that if I was anywhere near doing well, I knew exactly where to hit it: a hollow to the right of the green.

I could have gone anywhere from the dodgy lie that I had, but I really caught the ball solid and it bounced around the corner, over the bunker and just up short. I could either chip or putt it, but after years of playing links I didn't really think it was a chip, so I putted. It finished five feet from the hole and I pured it straight into the middle.

Score on hole: Par
Standing to par: -7

HOLE 16

Par 3
163 yards

So now I was on the 16th hole, the scene of Thomas Bjørn's three-out-of-a-bunker, which had ultimately cost him the title eight years earlier. I wasn't actually thinking about him when I stood over the tee shot, but I knew I didn't have to go for the flag, just in case I short-sided myself. I had to be sensible, so I knocked it into the middle and two-putted.

The crowds were really roaring and I looked up at the board and saw that I had a four-shot lead. It was going to take something spectacular, or disastrous on my part, for anybody to make that up.

I was thinking, 'Just play smart. You might not be renowned for your course management, but don't do anything stupid.'

Score on hole: Par
Standing to par: -7

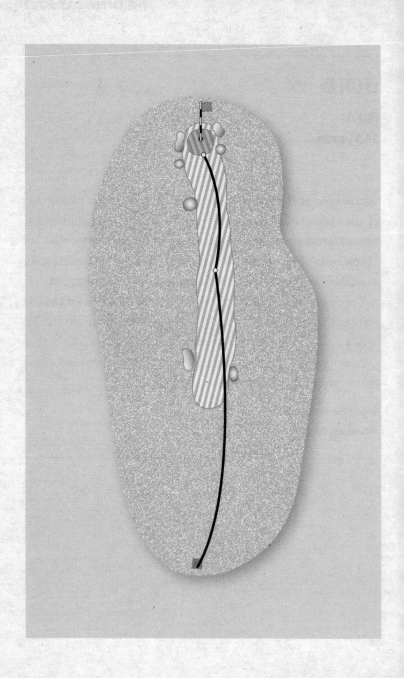

HOLE 17

Par 4
426 yards

Just two holes to play and I was definitely in the driving seat, but I still couldn't afford to let my mind stray too far because the last few holes of Open history are littered with the remains of broken dreams.

A nice drive and seven-iron approach left me reaching for the putter. Unfortunately, I would need it three times before moving on, but there wasn't too much damage because I still had shots to play with and just one hole left.

Score on hole: Bogey
Standing to par: -6

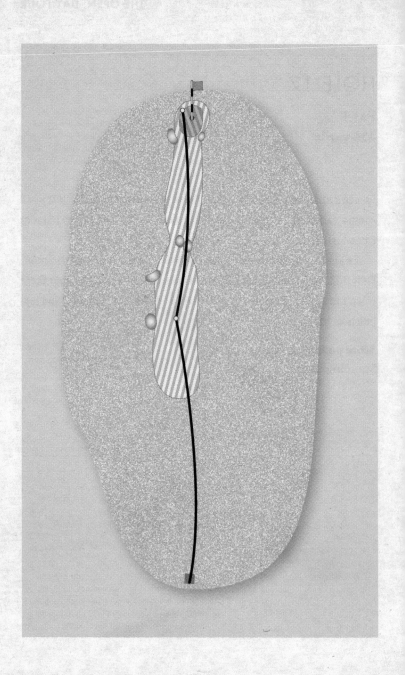

HOLE 18

Par 4
459 yards

I came to the 72nd and final hole of the tournament with a three-shot lead . . . and there isn't a golfer in the world who wouldn't relish that opportunity.

I could not afford to let my mind race ahead, though, so on the 18th tee I said to myself, 'Darren, this is the Open, and from all those years of practice and experience, you know that going into either of the two bunkers on the left could be a disaster, and there's a bit of rough on the right, so just give it one good swing. One good swing.'

Sure enough, I flushed it and found the fairway. I didn't actually pat myself on the back, but I knew the job was nearly done . . .

Score on hole: Bogey
Standing to par: -5

20

THE FINAL FAIRWAY

I walked off the 18th tee, twirling my TaylorMade R11 driver, and everybody was roaring and shouting. I still could not think about celebrating – only about the need to focus before hitting one more decent shot. Then I could enjoy it.

Dustin had already hit his tee shot into the rough so I knew it was going to be difficult for him to make the birdie he needed to give himself any chance at all.

I reached my ball and asked John what I had. I knew there were two places I couldn't hit it – bunker right and bunker left. As long as I had enough to carry everything and not go out of bounds way over the back then I'd be all right.

I aimed at a post at the back of the green, one of the out-of-bounds posts left of the flag, because I didn't want to be right. I absolutely nailed the five iron straight at my target and I knew it was fine. It would finish just off the left edge and I had three or four or, as it turned out, five from there to win the Open.

The realisation that I was close to winning really hit me as I walked down the final fairway. Thousands of people were roaring my name, shouting words of encouragement and congratulation.

Throughout that last round, in fact, the buzz from the crowd had been constant and on a couple of occasions I'd had to remind them that I wasn't the only one trying to win the Open. The reason I asked the crowd to be quiet whenever Dustin was about to play was simply because that's the way the game should be played. The roars and shouts for me were wonderful and I really, really enjoyed them, but when another player, a fellow professional, is about to hit his shot, it's only right that I should try to get the crowds to give him the respect they give me. It wasn't that I was embarrassed, not really. No, the crowds could not have been any better for me and whenever I did put my hands up for Dustin they went quiet straight away. They just got a bit over-exuberant at times. I loved every minute of it, though it was a little overwhelming after not having had that kind of support for a while.

Winning the Open was a lifelong dream, a constant ambition through adversity, and somehow I'd got there in the end. People had written me off, and now here I was walking up to the green and thinking, 'I've done it, I've actually done it. This is it. Finally. The one thing I wanted more than anything else in my sporting life – and I've done it.' It was an unbelievable feeling.

It was then that I thought about Heather. She was watching from above and, while proud of the achievement, was saying, 'I told you so.' But I knew she'd be more proud of our two boys watching at home.

I also thought about my family and friends, fiancée Alison and of course Chubby, who had been through everything with me and never stopped encouraging and picking me up when I was on the point of surrendering to the game.

It had been a long journey, and I could not have done it without them. There were those who expected me to break down, as I had after winning my final match at the K Club during the Ryder Cup, but I was in control. I am an emotional man, so if I hadn't felt a bit emotional it wouldn't be quite right, but I just about managed to hold on.

When I got to my ball, with 40 feet still to negotiate, I could not work out how many shots I had left to win. I knew I didn't have to two-putt, but whether it was three, four or five I wasn't quite sure. It must be three, no four, or was it five? But one thing I did know: I had more than two, so I could handle it.

I cleared all the thoughts from my head and said, 'Darren, just finish this off. Just do what you have to do and finish this off.'

I hit the first putt too hard, but I was making sure I didn't leave it short and risk rolling all the way back down. Dustin holed out, while I had a nine-footer and I was still trying to figure out if I had three or four. I hit the putt and left it two inches short. It didn't matter how many I had now because the next one was going in.

Someone shouted something from the crowd and I looked up and said something back, but to this day I can't remember what I said. It was probably along the lines of 'I think I can handle this from here.'

And just before I tapped in that career-defining two-inch putt – the greatest shot ever for me – I simply said to myself, 'I've done it at last.'

My closing 70 meant I was a three-stroke winner over Phil and Dustin and the oldest to collect the silver claret jug since Roberto de Vicenzo 44 years earlier.

And then something strange happened in my mind. I had a kind of flashback and all I could see was Greg Norman winning in 1993 and that multi-coloured shirt he wore when getting the better of Nick Faldo.

I wasn't quite lost for words, but initially I didn't get much further than saying, 'Incredible.' That just about summed up what I'd achieved. My childhood dreams were now reality and I wanted to drink it all in. This was headier stuff than alcohol, although there would be plenty of that later. All I'd done was my best and my best on the day was good enough.

I shook hands with everybody and gave John a hug and thanked him for everything he'd done, then I walked off to be greeted by familiar faces. Alison and my mum and dad were there together at the side. What nobody noticed was that as I walked towards them, Alison took a step back to let Mum and Dad give me a kiss and hug first. That was a touch of class which didn't surprise me. I went to give my dad a high five and completely missed, then hugged him and kissed my mum. It was so wonderful for me to have them there and for them to be able to share what they knew had been my lifetime's ambition. Then it was Alison's turn and then Chubby, who was in bits.

My good friend Davis Love III came up with tears in his eyes, gave me a big hug and said how pleased he was for me, and then

Phil and Amy Mickelson came over. Amy gave me a kiss and hug and I could tell that they were both genuinely pleased for me. What Phil said to me then will remain between the two of us, but publicly he said later, 'I'm really happy for him. He was one of the first people that called us, Amy and I. He couldn't have been a better person to talk to. We talked for a few hours a couple of times. He's a tremendous person and a very good friend, and I couldn't be happier for him. It was fun to try to make a run at him.'

The journey from the green to the recorder's hut is very much a blur, although I do remember it seemed to take an eternity. Before I could get through the door, good friend Miguel Angel Jiménez was there and Thomas Bjørn and Lucas Glover, all offering their congratulations. Then I left them to sign my card, knowing that life would never be the same.

Before the presentation there was a quick burst of television to do and I lost control of my emotions for the first time on one of them, but I quickly recovered as an ESPN mike came into range. I had been due to commentate for them over the weekend had I missed the cut so I apologised to the American viewers for playing too well to fulfil my obligations to them.

I was reminded that I shouldn't walk out for the presentation with my visor on, and Chubby handed me a piece of paper with a few bullet points for the champion's speech. I was told that nobody was sure how I wanted to play any reference to Heather and had left it for me to decide. So in the midst of everything, I was racking my brains for what I was going to say – in fact, not *what* I was going to say, but how I was going to get it out without hurting anybody's feelings or sounding too maudlin. I was scratching my head, because 95 per cent of the people there would have known my circumstances and I didn't want to get it wrong. I definitely wanted to mention Heather, and for more reasons than if I didn't I would be jumped on by the press.

After being announced in the time-honoured fashion as the Champion Golfer of the Year by Peter Dawson, Secretary of the R&A, I received the claret jug from Edward Demery, captain of Royal St George's, and walked towards the mike, still unsure what was going to come out of my mouth.

After making a few introductory remarks and thanking my family and those closest to me, I pointed up to the sky and said, 'And as some of you may know, there's somebody up there watching as well.'

The whole crowd erupted, roaring and shouting. It was an emotional moment, but it came out fine.

I was then able to thank all the other people who had to be mentioned. Although I had the bullet points for reference, the speech came from my heart and I was very pleased not to mess it up on global television. They were genuine words, which I wasn't reading, but I was also concerned not to make a gaffe, because I'd watched a few previous champions say the wrong thing.

Whatever had to be done now, I wouldn't be far removed from the pint of Guinness that Chubby had so kindly furnished me with.

* * *

The presentation ceremony and BBC television interview passed quickly, but the photographers wanted 'just one more' more than 200 times. I was perfectly happy to accommodate them. You never get tired of holding the claret jug. Then it was into the media centre for the champion's press conference, where it was standing room only.

Lawrence Donegan, then the *Guardian*'s golf correspondent, had the guts to hold his hand up and acknowledge that he was, as he put it, among 'the idiot golf writers out there who wrote you off'. I was delighted to be able to remind him of one phrase, written some time earlier, that had interested me, to say the least. He had said that I was on an 'inexorable slide towards golfing irrelevance'. It wasn't quite from the Tom McCollister book of things you wish you had never written – the late *Atlanta Journal-Constitution* journalist having said in the days before Jack Nicklaus's historic sixth win at Augusta that the Golden Bear was 'done, finished, through' – but it was pretty close.

I hadn't pinned the cutting on the fridge as Mr Nicklaus had, to inspire him to victory, but it was in my little black book at home and was definitely worthy of a PTAFW reference. Lawrence and I had actually sorted out our differences by this point and he had apologised when I'd won earlier in the year, but at the time I'd thought it was a pretty harsh and uncalled-for comment. I can take criticism if I think it is merited, but if I don't then I do take issue with it. But I was delighted to see Lawrence in the press conference and even more delighted to hear his opening line.

As the questions continued, I had to admit that there had been times when I had been completely fed up with the game and considered throwing the clubs away. Thankfully, I have always had a wonderful support system. In those desperate times, family, friends and Chubby have just said to me, 'Go and practise. Keep going, keep going, keep going.' That was the reason I was sitting in front of the world's press as Champion Golfer of 2011, proudly looking at the claret jug.

The questions came thick and fast. A lot of people went on about winning it at my twentieth attempt, but people play for ever and still don't win, so that was a bit of a silly one to me. The Open is the oldest and best tournament in the world and I would have thought so even if I hadn't won. It's what the game is all about. Every Open had been special to me, and although I'd had a couple of chances before and hadn't taken them, it is still what we all, particularly Europeans, strive towards. You can ask Mr Nicklaus, Mr Palmer, Mr Player, Mr Watson and even Tiger, and I bet they look on the Open as being the biggest of the four.

I was reminded that I'd promised to join Chubby on WeightWatchers after the Open. I was beginning to have second thoughts because, after all, I've always played better when I've been carrying a bit of condition . . . and perhaps it wasn't the best time for me to try to restrict my intake.

The Irish boys were looking for a home slant and one asked if I could put my finger on why such a small place as Northern Ireland had had three major champions in just thirteen months.

I reverted to that word again: 'incredible'. The country had produced fantastic champions in G-Mac and Rory, and I was just the older guy who'd come along behind them.

There were bound to be questions that would tug on the heart-strings and I was not disappointed. I held nothing back. In terms of what was going through my heart, I could only repeat what I'd been thinking when I had four to win from 40 feet. Heather had been watching, saying that she'd told me so. And she'd be proud, but I think she'd be more proud of the two boys.

To sit there next to the trophy, as the Open champion, meant the world to me. As I'd said in my speech, it had been a long and bumpy road to get there, and at 42 I was not getting any younger, but I had done it . . . finally. I'd gone out there, done my best, and my best was good enough to win. If I had come off and hadn't won, I could still have said I did my best. I could not have asked for anything else. I ask my two boys to do their best and that's what they do, so I think their dad should try to do the same. But whatever else happens throughout my career and life – as Phil Mickelson mentioned when he spoke to me after winning – I will always be an Open champion.

I got the impression that some of my inquisitors felt that I'd now be happy to enjoy what I'd done and quietly fade away into another Portrush or Abaco sunset. They did not know me. Asked what my remaining ambitions were, I looked at the jug and said I'd like another couple of them.

What was I going to do? Say that's it and retire? Of course not. Being the Open champion was just incredible – that word again

– so I'd go away, enjoy the moment, then reassess and set more goals. I was definitely not going to rest on this greatest moment of my career. I wanted to carry on working, practising, playing. After all, I had just proved that I could compete with the best players in the world.

As soon as the press conference was over, I headed for the R&A pavilion to meet the members. It was a journey of more than 300 yards, so there was plenty of time to phone the boys. The conversation went roughly along the lines I had expected. Tyrone was very pleased and proud and said he was going to tell everybody his dad was the Open champion. Conor simply asked what he could spend the money on. They were both very happy.

As the journey continued, I realised I was heading towards the group who had the power to make me an even happier man, if that was possible. It was my one of my biggest hopes that the R&A would recognise what three Ulstermen had achieved in thirteen months by awarding Royal Portrush the chance to stage an Open.

Actually, I would prefer to see it played at Royal Portrush every year. I knew the game's rulers would have to look at the logistics and infrastructure again, because their initial search had suggested they could not hold their championship there. It's very tough, but I do hope they find a way. The golf course is every bit as good as any of the Open venues and deserves to be on the roster. Hopefully they will figure a way around the logistics if they possibly can.

I have a huge amount of respect for Peter Dawson and his predecessor, Sir Michael Bonallack. They have a tough job running the R&A and they have done it very well. I think Peter, whose leg I pulled publicly regarding the Open going to Royal Portrush, was pleased with his Open champion, and being one of the older players on the Tour, I'd bumped into quite a few R&A members along the way. As I had a few drinks and spoke with them I got the impression that they too were pleased with what I had done a short time earlier.

Almost as satisfying for me as seeing my name on the jug was that while I was with the R&A they asked me to sign a poster that had been flown down from Prestwick Golf Club, where it resides, containing all the signatures of Open champions. What a privilege to be in this company. I found Fred Daly's signature and was proud to put mine immediately below my fellow Northern Irishman, who had won in 1947.

Later, I spoke quietly with Peter Dawson in the trophy room and he assured me that they were looking at the situation and knew exactly what was required for Royal Portrush to be awarded an Open. It's not just the course, but things like bedrooms, access, crowds and many other things. Until they decide that all criteria can be met then we can't do much more than hope. There were more than 180,000 people at Sandwich, and I'm sure we'd get that in Ireland, but there are so many other things to look at.

There were still plenty of stragglers left as we came out of the trophy room and made our way to the locker room, where another battery of cameras had to be addressed before I could finally relax.

*   *   *

It was now more than two hours since I'd looked up at the leader board and seen my name at the top with every shot played. Now I could enjoy it. ISM's hub house was only a five iron away from the main gates, so I was quickly into the swing of things.

I had no idea who was going to be there and the first person I saw was Selwyn Nathan, who had hung around to say well done before rushing off. His pyjamas had been changed for a pair of Black Watch tartan trousers and matching green tie and he gave me a big hug and said, 'I always knew you'd do it one day.'

There must have been at least 100 people in the house and I was greeted with a few shouts of congratulations before settling into what would turn out to be a session of quite monumental proportions.

I have never been so pleased to have my picture taken with so many different people in my life. I think somebody was dragging them in from the street, but it was fine by me. My parents and Alison were in much demand for interviews as the press sniffed out their follow-ups at this convenient watering hole so close to the course. And as the red wine flowed and the Guinness gushed, everybody got their quotes for a story I doubt any of them thought they would ever write.

Despite the copious quantities of alcohol consumed, it was, as celebration parties go, pretty civilised. Everybody was in good humour and behaving themselves and we were soon joined by the R&A's media corps, various players, sponsors and even the next-door neighbours – a fine initiative on someone's part, given the amount of noise that was coming from the revellers in the garden.

To be perfectly honest, it still hadn't sunk in properly that I'd won the Open, even when I was sitting down with Alison and Mum and Dad in the garden with the claret jug in the middle of the table.

Next thing, I looked up to see one of my best friends, Keith Maxwell, the professional at Sunningdale, coming through the door. He had driven all the way down from Surrey just to have one drink and then drive all the way back home. That's what friends do and I was delighted to be able to spend just a few moments of my finest hour with him in the garden.

That week I was also indebted to Dr Bob, of course, and I managed to have a word with him during the celebrations at the house. I told him that one of the most amazing things about the entire final day was that as soon as it got under way, I never really felt nervous at all. I told him I was delighted to have won a major, but I was also very happy to realise what I was capable of doing when I was in the right state of mind.

'I'm not too old to win these things and if I don't put pressure on myself I can win a bunch more,' I added. 'I don't want this to be the only one.'

Getty photographer Dave Cannon was there taking pictures and one of the things I'd said in my speech was that, with the R&A's permission, I'd like to fill the jug with some of the well-known Irish black stuff. Sure enough, a picture was taken that night of me in the garden with the jug to my lips and the score-board, still lit at the course, in the background.

It just shows that sometimes the camera can lie, because I was only pretending to drink from it. To my knowledge, not one drop of alcohol went into the jug in the time it was in my hands.

It was remarkable, really, or should I say incredible, that although I was quite hyper and it had been a long evening, I was nowhere near drunk. Yes, I was merrily drinking away – not excessively but drinking enough – yet the most I got was a buzz.

I was still more or less sober when a few of us finally retired to Chubby's house across the road, although sleep was not on the agenda. Fortunately, Alison, Garby and Dwarf No. 1 still had their drinking boots on, so I was not going to be left alone with the claret jug and my thoughts.

Sitting in the back garden, we began to sort out the world's problems over a couple of bottles of wine and did what people do when they have had a few and are just chilling. Garby offered us his Sir Michael Bonallack impersonation and formally presented me with the claret jug all over again, and at some point I took it upon myself to act as quizmaster as classics from the seventies blasted out from my iPhone. Name That Tune became a popular party pastime with our happy quartet.

As the clock's hands moved closer to daybreak, I remember sitting there, thinking that this was the greatest day of my life . . . and contemplating going to bed.

Not likely.

21

THE MORNING AFTER

So, freshly showered, smartly turned out, but not what you would call fully rested, I sat down at nine o'clock on the Monday morning to face the world's press again. I admitted to them that it still hadn't sunk in totally, even though I'd been staring at the trophy all night, apart from when I thought I'd lost it. I'd more or less figured out that it was mine, but I'd had to check from time to time to make sure my name was actually on it.

Knowing my history, my questioners wanted to know what I'd be spending the near-£1 million prize money on. The press boys seemed surprised when I said that now wasn't the time to look after myself, but to put a bit more aside for my boys' future. The only thing I'd wanted was to see my name on the trophy, and there it was. That meant more than any new toy. I was fortunate that the win would benefit me hugely financially, but what counted was seeing my name alongside golf's greats.

They wanted to know if I thought I'd changed over the years. I certainly believed I was a better player than I had been in my early thirties. I'd taken too much for granted then, but now I was definitely more appreciative of what sponsors do, what players need and how the Tour operated. I was much more switched on to everything that goes into a tournament.

Up to that point, I had not spoken much publicly about my caddie, John Mulrooney, so I was pleased to have the opportunity to set the record straight about John – he did a fantastic job at the Open – and the bizarre way we started working together just before the Iberdrola Open in Mallorca a couple of months earlier.

He had been due to caddie for David Howell there, but my ISM colleague was injured and John then picked up Maarten Lafeber's bag, only for him to get injured too. Meanwhile Ricci Roberts, Ernie Els's on-off caddie for many years, had begun working for me but couldn't make the trip to Mallorca. So Garby fixed up John, we won in Mallorca and I rang Ricci to say I couldn't really sack John after we'd just won together. Ricci was OK about it, and so John was with me when we got to Royal St George's. Strange how things work out.

John had worked on quite a few good bags before but was different in that he was quiet, which is unusual among caddies. But he was definitely a good one and although we'd had a bit of a blip in Scotland when he hadn't quite known how to deal with me on the last day when I was having a bit of a wobbly, he'd done a great job during the Open. He'd been spot on with his clubbing all week, and everything else for that matter.

Although I was feeling a little bit the worse for wear as the questions continued, I was smartly dressed and I thought my answers were understandable. But obviously there were some people, particularly in Ireland, who had other views. Some of the papers later hammered into me about having set a bad example and for turning up drunk for my press conference. They said it was pathetic that I'd been up drinking all night.

What a load of rubbish the do-gooders wrote. I will say just one thing on the subject. If I had to do it over again, would I change anything about it? Not one thing, not one bit, not for the world would I change a thing.

It was time to head home. I'd chartered a jet to get us all back and there was a bottle of champagne on board, so I had the hair of the dog. We were picked up at the airport and driven straight back to the boys. Tyrone was a bit teary like me, but Conor just grabbed hold of the claret jug and sat down with it. He cuddled it and nursed it and kept looking at it. He could have had a baby in his arms.

Then we went to our local, which is the Bayview Hotel in Portballintrae, complete with jug. There were only a few people there, but word spread fast and within twenty minutes the place was packed and everybody and his Irish wolfhound was having their picture taken with a trophy that had not seen that part of the world for sixty-four years, since Fred Daly brought it home.

At about 9 p.m. I started to fall asleep at the table, and Alison – what a sensible girl she is – spirited me out of the place, took me home and tucked me in. I'd woken at 8 a.m. on the Sunday morning, so it had been almost a day and a half since I'd last slept – not a bad session, I may say.

The homecoming the following day at Royal Portrush was quite some celebration as well. The roads were lined with people and there must have been a few thousand inside the gates, but the same security guys who had taken care of Graeme McDowell and

Rory McIlroy after their major wins were in charge and they were getting quite used to it by now.

Deputy First Minister Martin McGuinness was among the VIPs in attendance and it seemed that everybody wanted a photograph, including the policemen who were there just to make sure nothing got out of hand.

There were so many photographers, reporters and television cameras that you'd have thought I'd won the triple of the Open, Wimbledon and the Boat Race, but they all managed to get their picture or story before I was finally able to sneak off to the Harbour Bar in Portrush to top up.

That night I treated everybody to a free bar, and what a party it was, but my sensible head was screwed on again. I had to go to London the following morning to collect a £2 million sponsors' cheque from Mr Mike Ashley, owner of Newcastle United and a multitude of sporting-goods shops and companies, including Dunlop Slazenger, who had very kindly agreed to donate that sum to my bank balance should I ever win a major. I'm sure he had thought his money was safe.

I wasn't expecting the amount of media interest following my win. It wasn't as if I was a new kid on the block. I'd been out there a long time, but the media commitments were unbelievable. It didn't seem possible that there were still photographers out there who hadn't got a snap already, but I had plenty of press to do before I was finally able to sit back, relax and reflect a little.

I thought about the last round and the breaks that went my way at crucial points. I've always been realistic in trying to assess whether I've deserved to win or needed to get lucky to win. I've always felt better if I've deserved it. Winning lucky doesn't feel as good. When I reflected on that Sunday, I didn't think that it was a case of being lucky, but of the course giving me a bit back.

If my putting had been anything close to matching my ball-striking the previous day, then I would have gone into the last round holding a four- or five-shot lead, not just one. Golf takes and gives back, I feel. Four or five prime years of my career were more or less put on hold through Heather being ill. I never felt sorry for myself in that period because that situation is going to be a struggle for anybody, from whatever walk of life, and you have to face it and deal with it the best you can. Now I was thinking that golf had given me something back.

I wouldn't say I was a religious man by any stretch of the imagination, but sometimes things happen that you can't explain, both good and bad. I'd had bad and now this was a bit of good, so I didn't think I got lucky. I suppose I believe a little bit in destiny, but I also believe in a work ethic – that if you put your heart and soul into something, at some stage you will get paid back for what you do. What happened at Sandwich was payback for all the long, lonely hours spent hitting balls.

I started thinking about the game and sport in general and just how much it teaches you. I'm delighted I grew up in a sporting environment, because it is very character-developing, and particularly golf, where you mingle with older people much earlier than you would normally do. I'm so pleased that both my boys enjoy the game, because it teaches you so much about honesty, integrity, etiquette, manners, communication and also respect for both the game and your opponent.

22

RORY, LEE, CHUBBY AND ME

The first time I saw Rory McIlroy I knew. The potential in the 13-year-old was that obvious. It was at the Darren Clarke Foundation weekend in Dublin and here was this small, thin kid from home with a fresh face and ridiculously good talent.

Rory was just so keen and couldn't play enough. You could see how much he wanted it and he was barely a teenager. It was so good to see. He loved to show off his game. He wasn't bragging, he was just showing you his spark, and I knew that would take him wherever he wanted, as long as his work ethic stayed high.

The golf world is littered with the skeletons of talent that never matured or lost its way, but with Rory it was different. He had not only the talent but also the desire and when you put those two together, it's going to work out somewhere down the line. And when you factor in a propensity for hard work, you know it's going to happen sooner rather than later.

I'm not being wise after the event because, although I was always careful not to place too much pressure on such slim shoulders in public, I was saying in private that golf's next major talent had been discovered in our tiny little land.

Rory had my telephone number at a very early age and I was always available to give him advice or a helping hand if he wanted it. I never forced anything on him, but I was always at the end of a phone. The thing with Rory was that I knew that he would do everything the way that he wanted to. He didn't call that often and he didn't have to. He knew. He was and is his own man.

Rory's amateur career glittered from start to finish and he had only just celebrated his 17th birthday when he topped the world amateur rankings in 2007. It was his signal that he was ready for the professional ranks. When it came to having some kind of management structure behind him, Rory had known Chubby for a long time. He'd seen how the big man operated and he felt comfortable that it was a match that would fit for him too.

When Rory did turn professional it was late in the 2007 season and he had only seven invitations in which to earn enough money to gain his playing privileges for the following season. Remarkably, he needed just three, although it turned out that what he earned in the first two would have been enough. A couple of years later Rory won for the first time.

What he let slip at Augusta in the spring of 2011, when a huge lead disappeared on a fateful final day, must have been not just disappointing but also gut-wrenching. Lesser talents might have faded away into obscurity for a while. For him to bounce back in the manner that he did at Congressional in the US Open two months later – with a record-winning score of 16 under – was nothing short of sensational. Rory simply crushed everybody. Eight shots was the biggest winning margin in a long time. To dominate like that at the age of 22 was just fantastic, it really was.

I was not the least bit shocked when he knocked off his first major. Nor when he won the USPGA Championship at Kiawa in August 2012, also by eight strokes. There will be others, of that there can be no doubt. I enjoy Rory, I enjoy playing with him and being his friend, and I particularly enjoy watching how he hits the golf ball. It's wonderful. Do I still want to play and compete against him and try to beat him? Of course I do. He'll probably beat me more often than I'll beat him, but I've still got a few shots left in the bag.

Rory seemed perfectly happy at ISM for several years, but then it changed quickly and unexpectedly in the late summer of 2011, just after he and I had had won our major championships. Sometimes relationships just don't go the right way and it looks like that's what happened, but I have no real idea because we have never talked about it. Rory obviously decided that he wanted to go a different route. I was as shocked and surprised as anybody when Chubby called to tell me.

There were no ill feelings whatsoever. Rory's a big boy now. It's his life, his job, his decision. I was just very lucky that I got to spend a little time with him.

There is not the slightest chance that I would ever leave Chubby's stable, but that's not to say we haven't had our differences. We've fallen out a handful of times. Nothing particularly serious, though.

One incident occurred during practice for the Alfred Dunhill Links quite a few years ago when we were discussing how many shots he should receive as I partnered then England cricket captain Michael Vaughan against Chubby and Lee Westwood.

When Chubby negotiates, he doesn't agree until he has been given at least two more shots than he is supposed to get. The deal and the bet were struck, but when it came to Chubby's turn to play he moved to the forward tees. Not only was he looking for extra shots but also extra yardage. I did not take too kindly to this at all and told him all bets were off. It was just a bit of petulance, but I didn't speak to him for a month.

Now, Chubby is just as stubborn as me, but in our twenty-plus years together he's certainly given me far more rollickings than I've given him and I must admit that for the most part I've deserved them. In fact, I can't remember why we fell out on other occasions, but it was probably over nothing more than our joint stubbornness. Chubby works under the adage that rule number one is that the boss is always right and rule number two is that when the boss is wrong refer to rule number one.

To be fair, although Chubby thinks he's always right, he is right about 95 per cent of the time, and you can be 100 per cent certain that all he is trying to do is something for his players' best interests. All in all, I wouldn't be where I am without him. Chubby's management company and my achievements have grown together and I trust him implicitly. I have absolutely no idea how much commission I have paid ISM and I've never asked because I have that much trust in him and them. It's irrelevant, because I couldn't have done what I have without them.

In golfing terms, I don't think he has ever had to reprimand me, because he did a such good job of teaching me how to deal with sponsors and pro-am partners and about time-keeping and smartness. Right from the off, Chubby always stressed the importance of being good to those who were or had the potential to be good to me. It didn't matter how much money they were paying for me to represent them, whatever I did I had to ensure that I gave them value for money. I think that's what I've managed to do.

I don't think I've ever had any unhappy sponsors and that's down to me doing the right thing and Chubby matching the sponsor to me. There have been offers we have turned down simply because Chubby has felt they were not right for me. His decisions in that respect have always been 100 per cent correct.

We have had a lot of heart-to-hearts when it's come to our private lives. We have both had pretty tempestuous ones from time to time. I've tried to help him and he's tried to help me through thick and thin.

When I won the Open, people talked about the possibility of a 'Chubby Slam'. With Charl Schwartzel having been fitted for a green jacket at Augusta, Rory making history at Congressional and then me at Royal St George's, it meant that ISM had the first three majors of the year. If someone was going to win the fourth, then I could think of no more deserving a player than my good friend Lee Westwood. He'd been knocking on the door for so long, it would be wonderful to see him win one. Unfortunately, American Keegan Bradley would deny him at the US PGA in

Atlanta, but I'm sure there will be at least one for him before he hangs up his spikes.

Lee joined ISM about a couple of years after I did and we weren't anything more than nodding acquaintances for another couple after that. But more and more, as we both started winning and developing, a friendship came with it and we started playing practice rounds and then travelling together. People have often asked how close we are and I can best demonstrate it by saying one thing: If I was in trouble, I'd call Lee.

Of all people playing today who have not claimed one of the game's biggest prizes, I think Lee deserves something. Right now it must have been tough for him, with Rory and then me winning. But if I were a gambling man, which I'm not, I would have a substantial bet on Lee winning a major or majors at some point. And with the physical condition he's in, he has plenty of time to do it.

I'm also close to Tiger, but I don't get much chance to socialise with him, for the most part because when our paths do cross it's normally at a major or WGC event, when we both have to be focused on what we are doing.

Tiger's another who has had a fair share of trauma in his life and I am delighted that the fight he has shown to come out the other side has started to pay off for him. Sometimes it takes a while to get some balance back in your life when you've been through something as difficult as divorce. But it's great to see him back in the winner's circle again. That can only be good for the game.

23

TRYING TO GET IT RIGHT

If any golfer tells you they don't suffer from nerves, you know they are telling porky pies. I'm often nervous and never more so than at the Ryder Cup, where you have the added burden of responsibility to other members of your team, your country and your continent. When you're nervous you miss putts you should hole, you hit shots you shouldn't hit. The test is how you control those nerves and how you react to them.

On occasions I've come home feeling as if I've really messed up, but that's all part of the game. I've had my share of pain and that's why seeing the other side of things at the 2011 Open was worth all the torture. But whatever I've been through, I've nearly always managed to control myself, particularly in public.

I know of golfers who have had a sudden brainstorm when driving away from a tournament and have pulled over and thrown all their clubs into a river one by one. Then there are those who take great joy in heading off with their putters fastened to their bumpers and others who snap clubs over their thighs in the middle of a round.

I can honestly hold my hands up and say that I rarely break clubs, although I have dismantled the odd tee box. Everyone's attacked a tee marker at least once in their career. I admit I have used bad language too frequently, but it's been born out of frustration, and when I have reached breaking point it has generally been the putter that has felt the full force of my frustration.

Amateurs play the game from tee to green, but professionals invariably work back from the green to the tee. If you're putting well, the rest of the game is easier. You don't mind missing greens with your irons because you know that there is every chance you're going to get up and down. And you don't mind missing a fairway off the tee because you feel your putter is going to bail you out eventually.

When the shortest club in the bag misbehaves, however, its owner is likely to follow suit from time to time. One such occasion occurred at Valderrama in the late 2000s. My problems on the green were so bad that I'd been forced to try a belly putter, which goes against all my traditional values. I persisted with it all week, but to no avail, and when I went to get changed on the Sunday afternoon I placed it against my locker and put my foot straight through it.

I didn't think there was a funny side at the time, nor was I particularly proud of myself, and I certainly wasn't aware that I was being watched by anyone but my caddie, who had the good sense to keep quiet while I was going through the ritual of breaking and binning. But as I threw the now two-piece putter into the nearest bin, an explosion of laughter cut through the room. José María Olazábal thought it all extremely amusing.

Yet for the most part, I've tried to do the sensible thing and I have often given clubs to kids at the side of the green when I feel they are of no more use to me. I've usually been too wary of damaging the game's reputation, so I've publicly kept my emotions in check.

One thing I'm never wary of is speaking my mind. I'm not political, but I will stand up for what I believe in. I'm on the European Tour's Tournament Committee and have been for quite some time, and if I think something is wrong I will make my point. I have no personal issues because everything I do on the committee is for the betterment of the European Tour.

One of the things that I take great exception to is slow play. I'm more of the find-it-and-hit-it type of golfer, so I'm not keen on playing with anybody who takes an age to play their shots. The few fines I've incurred on the Tour have been for withdrawing late from tournaments, but I have also been warned a couple of times about slow play. On both occasions I went ballistic with the referee because it wasn't my fault. The problem is that it's the group rather than the individual that gets warned and I don't agree that that's the right procedure.

A lot of well-known top players have been slow in the past, but when a referee comes along it's not just them who is affected. The entire group is, and I take exception to that. The guy they are checking speeds up, but the other two, who have done nothing wrong, feel that they have to speed up too because they're on the clock. That's nonsense to me.

It happens a lot on the Tour. We do police ourselves to a certain extent and I've never been slow to point out to playing partners when we have lost our position on the course. I tell them we'd better make up time or we'll be put on the clock. Officials say they can't put just the slow players on the clock because that would be discriminating. To which I have a very short and succinct reply.

I don't advocate a softly-softly approach to slow play; in fact, completely the opposite. We all know who the slow players are – the referees know who they are – so why not put them on the clock on the first tee and fine them when they play slowly? And as soon as you've fined them a couple of times, dock them shots. Only when players are penalised shots regularly will you begin to see a real difference.

This modern-day scenario of a three-ball taking five hours is disgraceful. You only have to go to your local club to see young kids standing behind the ball taking two or three practice shots. They're doing it because the pros do it.

Some of the bigger names have got away with it for a long time, while some of the young kids coming out have been fined. That is harsh. Everybody should have to adhere to the same rules, but there are those who set their own agendas and pace of play and that affects the rest of the field. Dock them shots no matter who they are.

I feel equally passionately about rule-breakers, and I use that term because 'cheats' is a very strong word and one we are careful not to use on the Tour in these litigious times.

Unfortunately, there have been occasions on which rules have been broken and that's a very sad part of the game. For me it is a hard thing to take, because I believe the game should be played in the same spirit by everybody, with honesty and truthfulness. Golf is one of the few sports left in which it all comes down to the player. You have to ask yourself, 'Did I or did I not break the rules?'

When somebody transgresses and denies it, I don't know how they can live with their conscience. If it were me, I couldn't sleep. You're lying to yourself. I can see that the temptation is there because of the huge amounts of money we're playing for now, but if you do it once and get away with it, however small the offence, then some will be tempted to do it again. Where do you stop? Once you cross that line you can never come back. All the guys on the Tour know who breaks the rules. The players know, the caddies know, and the offenders get a reputation that they never lose. All their days on the Tour, they never lose it.

Rule-breaking is the dirty side of our game, but thankfully it doesn't happen that often, indeed very rarely. But when it does happen, it's rightly dealt with more severely than it has ever been. We have a responsibility because we are representatives of the game. We are on television and what we do will be imitated at the local club. Then again, I don't believe in trial by television – that can be unfair. The simple reason is that only the top players and those at the head of the field are shown on the box. It's not a general trial – it's selective – and that can't be right.

What's happening more and more these days is that players are much quicker to report what they've seen if they spot somebody breaking the rules. I don't think I've ever played with anybody who has broken the rules deliberately, but there have been occasions when I've mentioned to tournament directors that they might want to take a second look at something.

After that it's up to the player to answer for what he's been accused of and if he denies it, it can be difficult to prove otherwise, particularly when it's one person's word against another. Accusing somebody of breaking the rules deliberately is a tough and serious matter, but if there's enough evidence there, then they should be punished accordingly.

24

THE REAL ME

There are plenty of popular misconceptions about me and many revolve around drink. To listen to some you'd think I crawled home every night, but while I admit to a liking for the black stuff and fine red wine, I rarely imbibe more than I can handle, and it never interferes with my professional life. On the road, I can go for weeks without touching a drop and if I do go on a serious bender it is always well away from a tournament. People who think I'm a party guy who plays golf and then goes straight to the pub do not know the true Darren Christopher Clarke.

So what is the real me?

One of my biggest pluses is also one of my biggest negatives, in that my desire and determination, admirable qualities for the most part, sometimes get in the way of what I am trying to achieve. I want things so badly that although my attitude has driven me to the highest of highs, it has also taken me to the lowest of lows. And I find it very difficult to deal with the lows. I'm either up or down. When I'm up I'm fine, and when I'm down I'm best left to my own devices. There's not a lot in the middle.

Without that drive I don't think I would have achieved half of what I have. If I'm going to do something, I do it properly – and in golf it is always within the rules of the game. But the desire can be so great that it makes me intolerant of imperfection.

If you ask people outside the game to list the golfers most dedicated to their profession, I doubt that my name would figure too highly, but ask anybody inside the game and they will tell you that I am often the last to leave the range. But therein lies the problem. Because I work very hard, I expect results to follow, and golf doesn't work like that. Sometimes it goes the other way and that frustrates the hell out of me.

Success and failure in this fantastic but infuriating game can rest on one lucky bounce; one kind ricochet off a tree back into the fairway or deeper into the woods; one holed putt against a lip-out; one hop left into safety or right into water. There are so many variables and at times I have struggled to cope with them.

Consistency has never been one of my strong points and that's the way I've always been. I'm a streaky player. When I'm on, I'm as good as anybody; when I'm off, I can't beat Chubby. The trouble is I know how well I can play and I want to play like that every week. It just does not happen and never will.

That same desire, determination – talent, if you will – is also the reason I get so low and fed up with the game. At times I am tempted to break the clubs or throw them away, but then I remind myself that losing my head and misbehaving on the golf course wouldn't make my boys very proud, would it? And that's why I don't do it, in public anyway.

I have let my attitude get the better of me on many occasions. I know I shouldn't have done, but I have. I get very angry with myself, and in those circumstances I am not a particularly nice person to be around. I rarely fall out with anybody other than myself, however. In all my years on the Tour, I haven't really had a big bust-up with many people, although I once threatened to thump a major champion who had hit a ball way too close to my head.

I've always struggled to deal with failure and in golf you have to deal with an awful lot of it. A golfer is only as good as his last result, unfortunately for me. I should be more relaxed. I should be happier and I'm not, because I crave success – not from a material point of view, not for recognition, but for myself. That hunger has been to the detriment of earlier relationships, including my relationship with Heather at times, because golf to me is all-consuming. It shouldn't be, but it is.

I frequently ask myself, why am I doing this, why am I working away at this, why am I pushing myself to the limits, why am I doing it all over and over again? It's driven me totally mad at times. There's a saying that the definition of insanity is doing the same thing over and over again and expecting different results. Well, I've done all the right things – the practice, the gym, sports psychologists, coaches – over and over again, but the results rarely satisfy me.

My good friend Keith Maxwell once told me that before anybody can bounce back up they have to get right to the bottom. That's been my career. I've seriously thought about packing it in on several occasions, but those feelings have not lasted, because I love the game so much. I absolutely detest it at times too, I really do, and I sometimes wonder about the futility of it all, but I just can't give it up. It's a drug to me.

The challenge keeps me going. It's me against the golf course and the outcome solely depends on me, nobody else. In team sport you can have an off day and your team can carry you; in tennis you're against an opponent who can have a bad day and you have a great day; but in our game what anybody else does has no relevance. It's solely down to us, because we have no control over what anybody else does. If we have an off day, we have an off day and that's that – which is why it's always been a mentally demanding sport.

You need to be in a good frame of mind all the time, and I'm not. I'm frequently hacked off because I'm so hard on myself and it's all born out of frustration. My life couldn't be any better than it is right now, with a lovely wife and family. My boys are good, my life's good, Alison's great – but does that stop me getting fed up when I have no reason to be? Not at all.

And then there is the other Darren Christopher Clarke.

I'm a giver in a world of takers. I try to look after people who have helped me and I like to be very generous towards them. I never forget when people have been good to me and it's fair to say I also never forget when anybody's been bad.

I've never actively sought a celebrity lifestyle. I've been materialistic because I've been in a position to afford the things I've dreamt of. I had pictures of Lamborghinis on my bedroom wall as I was growing up, and when I could afford one I bought one. I've been very good to myself, but I also take great pleasure in helping out my friends.

As Butch Harmon once said to me, 'You don't see any hearses pulling a safe.' Well, you're definitely not going to see mine pulling one. Sometimes I'm generous to the point of stupidity, but I get great enjoyment from it. I've always done it and for nobody more than my family. I like to share a bit of happiness and that's why I employ all my family.

My three main hobbies outside golf are cars, wine and fly fishing. I indulge in them way too much but I enjoy doing it. I work hard, so I play hard. What's the point in working so hard if I can't do that? Mind you, sometimes I've rewarded myself a little too much in comparison to what I've achieved and Chubby has had to rein me in. It was once said that I lived a major championship lifestyle without the major. To be honest, I probably got that from Chubby himself.

Which brings me to sarcasm, the lowest form of wit, but in the company we keep on the Tour, the only form. We're constantly trying to get one over each other, particularly Lee Westwood, and wind-ups are always par for the course.

You can be sure that whatever you give, it's going to come back in spades and particularly now that I am living back home in Northern Ireland. All my friends understand my sense of humour and I get plenty back, plenty. One of their favourites is to ask me what I'm doing the following Saturday, knowing that I'll definitely be playing the first two rounds of the next tournament, but not necessarily the Saturday or Sunday.

I didn't have that when I lived behind the big gates in Longcross. I'd get a bit from Keith Maxwell and Paul McGinley, but I didn't allow an awful lot of people to get close to me. When you've been let down you tend to keep people at arm's length. And I'm not a celebrity golfer; it's not me, just not my thing. It's nice to get invited to one or two events now and again, and I do have some celebrity friends, but throughout my career I've tended to surround myself with what I would call regular, normal people. If I had the choice between doing the normal thing or going the celebrity route, I'd choose normal every time.

I've done quite a few personality tests, including the Myers-Briggs, and those results indicate I'm an introvert, but people think I'm an extrovert. I am shy and will never go into a room first if there is an option. I fly under the radar as much as possible. Yet that will never have come across, particularly in light of some of the outfits I've worn at tournaments, although I'd like to think I am a touch more conservative these days.

One thing that has been a constant throughout my career and for most of my life is that when it comes to shopping and spending, I have few rivals. My excesses often have to be seen to be believed. If I said I once bought sixty pairs of Calvin Klein underpants, would you believe me? Didn't think so, but I did. Or forty pairs of trousers on the same day from the same shop? Yes, I did. Or thirty belts? Yes, that's me.

I've had fifteen Ferraris, three Lamborghinis and an assortment of Jags, Bentleys, Mercedes, BMWs and Porsches. The most

cars I've ever had at once was seven and I'll admit that was a little excessive. I'm more sensible now. I definitely have to be in Portrush, otherwise I'd risk being known as that 'flash ******
who lives on top of the hill'.

It was not the least bit funny to me at the time, but I can't help laughing now about a story that revolves around my gizmo and speed fetish. Now, I've had plenty of different vehicles, but none so exotic, shall I say, as the £35,000 trike I ordered from the German company Boom Trikes. I was quite excited when this big, beautiful machine arrived after being imported into Birmingham and then driven down to Longcross. I was all smiles when my new toy with the shining black chrome and Volkswagen 2-litre engine was unloaded from the transporter. It looked absolutely brilliant and I couldn't wait to get behind the handlebars, but before the delivery men would let me take control they took me for a test drive outside the gates. They carefully showed me how everything worked and then brought me back after ten minutes.

The gates were just about to open to let them take the transporter out when I went for my first drive – a calamitous fifteen yards. I jumped into the driving seat and had no sooner settled in and started up than my foot slipped off the brake. The trike took off straight into a flower bed, through a small tree, and didn't stop until it crashed into the side of the house. I have never heard laughter like it, although not from me. I felt like an absolute muppet.

So within minutes of unloading, the dealer and driver were just as quickly reloading it and driving it back to Birmingham to have new front forks and wheel fitted. When it came back, I did have several rather more successful drives on it – before Sam Torrance made me an offer I couldn't refuse.

The lifestyle I've had, I dreamed about as a kid, even though there was nothing wrong with the modest lifestyle I had growing up. My dreams were big not small because I have always felt that if you don't aim high enough, you will invariably come up short.

This may take some believing, but I've never known how much money I've had in the bank, although occasionally I've known how little there was when Chubby's said, 'For heaven's sake, Darren, stop spending.'

My greatest extravagance was definitely the private jet I owned with Lee. It cost us something like $12 million, with annual running costs of $2 million, and we had it for about ten years. The running costs were ridiculous, but it was a great idea at the time. We were travelling a lot together because our itineraries were similar and it worked for us. But when Heather got sick, my schedule got out of sync with Lee's, so when he used it, it cost him double and the same for me when I used it. We couldn't split the bills any more and that's when it stopped working, but there was always a nice buzz walking up the stairs to your own jet.

I still fly private occasionally because it's much quicker and easier, with no baggage restrictions, and it's faster through security. Looking back now, I know it was an extravagance, but that was when I was playing an awful lot of golf in Europe and America. Over the course of a year, it gave me an extra week with the kids and that was priceless.

Nowadays I'm just as happy going down to Belfast and getting on easyJet. I'm a lot more sensible than I used to be and some of that has been forced on me, because when Heather passed away I had to sit down and figure everything out. Thankfully, Alison has been wonderful for me in that respect. She's a business-woman who knows far more about the value of money than I do. She's helped me curb that foolish, excessive side.

I did enjoy the high life for a while when I was in London, but circumstances changed and although London was the best place to be based for my golf, it wasn't for my life. London and Portrush are chalk and cheese. London is a massive, wonderful city, full of the best things in life and all kinds of people and characters, whereas small-town Portrush has just a few of the nice things in life, but is full of all the best people.

One of my favourite rituals when I'm home is meeting my dad and brother-in-law Davy and friends like Derek McFaull, Clive Kennedy, Damien Clyde and David Gilliland at 5 p.m. every Friday at the Bayview Hotel in Portballintrae. Six or seven of us sit at a round table to enjoy a couple of pints and a lot of craic. It's boys' time, and that's something I never had in London.

I had a lovely house there in a beautiful area and Queenwood was a fantastic course, but there was no mates thing going on – people I could have a pint with and who would bring me back to earth if I was getting above my station. It seemed to be more of a transient area. People came there for their jobs and then moved away without putting down roots, so there was no real sense of community.

Although I adore the house I have in the Bahamas, there is no place like home and that home is Portrush. When you come from Ulster, there's always the question about whether you are British or Irish. I loved London and I've loved representing Ireland, but when people ask what I am, I'm just proud to say that I'm from Northern Ireland. It's home.

One thing that hasn't changed since I returned home is the colour of my hair – it's natural for one of the few times in my life. I thought that turning 40 was the perfect time to go back to my own roots, as it were. It was one of two things I'd told myself I'd do when I reached that milestone. The second was that I would buy myself a Rolls-Royce, but when the day came, I didn't feel it was time to hit the road in a Rolls. That's now been put back to when I'm 50, but when I get there, I'll probably put it off again. One day, though.

As for my dress sense, it's been an ever-changing process. I've always had a bit of an interest in clothing, although sometimes I have been accused of getting dressed in a darkened room. I will admit that occasionally I have been advised to wear something which I was assured looked good, but in retrospect was anything but. When that's happened, it's usually been at a time when I've been working out in the gym and in good shape and so could carry off most things reasonably well. The trouble with that is, as Chubby occasionally reminds me, I play better fat.

I may have come across at times as the extrovert I'm not. I just do it to be a bit different. I'm a traditionalist in a lot of ways, but in others I'm not. I doubt you'll ever find me in khaki trousers and white shirt. I don't want to be the same as everyone else, but I don't want to stand out either. I usually dress smartly off the course and I'm quite comfortable in jacket and tie. It's part of my business and what I have to do. Many sponsors have paid me a lot over the years and I think I owe it to them to dress well. And that goes for evening time as well, if I'm out and about.

I've had some great sponsors throughout my career. TaylorMade have been fantastic on the golf side, while none has been more generous from a commercial point of view than Barclays. I've done days for them all over the globe and I got to know Bob Diamond, their former CEO. It has been my pleasure to spend many hours in the company of successful and influential people and I love nothing more than tapping into their knowledge and experience. I have never been afraid to ask their opinions in the hope that I can implement what I've learned in my world. There may not be many parallels between business and golf, but it seems to me that one is the mental aspect of coping with many varied situations.

I was with Barclays for eight years, but with the downturn in the world's economies and the problems in the banking sector, combined with a downturn in my fortunes on the course, they decided it was time to move on. Ironically, almost as soon as the Barclays sign had been taken from my visor and replaced with a TaylorMade one, I was walking down the fairways of Royal St George's towards my greatest hour, watched everywhere in the golfing world.

I'm sure the irony was not lost on Bob and he kindly sent me his congratulations. I hope he laughed at my response.

25

ALISON

It was a November day in 2009. My face was as long as a fortnight but would quickly wear a smile just as broad. My life was about to change again.

An assortment of players, including Lee, G-Mac, Rory and a pack of rats, as caddies are affectionately known, were sitting in the JW Marriott in Hong Kong prior to going to the airport. If anybody was talking to me they were only getting monosyllabic answers in return. To say I was glum was putting it mildly. I'd finished 61st in the Race to Dubai and only the top 60 qualified for the season-ending Dubai World Championship.

G-Mac tried to raise my spirits by telling me about this girl I might have heard of and might fancy getting to know. Her name was Alison Campbell and she'd been Miss Northern Ireland and was now the owner of a very successful model agency. Give her a call, he urged.

I hadn't heard of Alison, and instead of giving her a call I sent her a text just before I had to turn off my phone for the long flight home. When I landed at Heathrow, there was a positive message on my iPhone and we met in London the following Friday. The next day she accompanied me to television broadcaster Eamonn Holmes's 50th birthday celebrations at Old Trafford.

The attraction to Alison was instant and for far more reasons than the purely physical. I found her fantastic company and she was clearly extremely clever, far too clever for me. If I had any reservations, they did not surround Alison, because I am as sure as anybody possibly can be about her and our future together. I realised very quickly that what we had was both different and special. But there were other people to factor into the relationship.

Alison has two boys: Stuart, who lives and works in San Francisco, and Philip, who is at Manchester University. As they are that bit older than mine, she has been through the whole process of kids growing up, so I was sure that would help when it came to Tyrone and Conor. And the fact that she is very media-savvy made me realise that she would be able to cope with all the extra attention our association was bound to attract.

My boys have to be my number-one priority and will always be, so if they weren't going to be happy about their dad's relationship, then it would have made everything quite difficult. They'd had a tough time, and had come through it exceptionally well in the circumstances, but I couldn't gauge what would develop once they were introduced to Alison. I need not have worried. They got on well from the off and now they think the world of her.

Despite being independent and having her own life, she still makes a lot of time for me. To be honest, she probably puts herself out for me more than I do for her. Our relationship developed quickly and Alison was about to go to a party with her models in Belfast just before the Christmas of 2010 when I proposed. I was absolutely delighted when she accepted.

We were married in the Bahamas on the beach in Abaco with about twenty guests the week after the 2012 US Masters. All of us were dressed in white – shorts for me – and it was a great week with family and friends. We were delighted when G-Mac, who had brought us together, was able to join us, along with his girl-friend, Kristin Stape.

Since Royal St George's, the marriage-holiday was one of many memorable moments off the course. In contrast, there have been very few on it. It's the old story of pushing myself to play better instead of relaxing and enjoying myself. That's when I play my best golf, when I'm relaxed, but I just can't sit back and I won't let myself rest. It's a catch-22 situation I find myself trapped in again and again.

Now I must look forward. I still love the game and it has been unbelievably good to me. I've won more than twenty times and though I feel I should have won a lot more, it's given me the opportunity to travel the world and play in fantastic tournaments. I've won some of the biggest golfing events there are and made many friends.

So what else has golf given me? It's given me highs and lows and a lifestyle I could only dream of when I was growing up. It's also given me the opportunity to promote breast cancer aware-ness and research, and to develop junior golf in Ireland through my foundation and school. What I'm basically trying to do is give something back to the kids and Irish golf in general because the Golf Union of Ireland was so good to me.

The Darren Clarke Foundation operates separately from the Darren Clarke Golf School, which is in Antrim at Greenmount College, where kids can spend two years sampling what golf is all about, as well as gaining a full-time university-recognised qualification, instead of having to go to America for the collegiate system. We cover every aspect and one of the most important things I try to get across at both the foundation and school is that everybody should play the game in the right way. The foundation's aims are to introduce kids to golf so that they can experience the qualities of honesty, integrity, responsibility, fair play and equality. I also try to pass on some of my knowledge and experiences. The highlight is the Champions Weekend, when, as the name implies, all the qualifiers are champions who've won provincial or national titles.

Professionals sometimes lose sight of the fact that it is a game. I have always tried to play it in the right way. There's give and take, there's sportsmanship, and at the end of the day the best man wins. Shake their hand on the 18th green, have a drink with them afterwards and say, 'Thank you very much for the game.' That's what I try to instil in all the kids who come through my school and my foundation. It's a game. It's not life or death. Play hard, but enjoy it at the same time.

My parents sacrificed everything for me, when they couldn't really afford it, and although it's a completely different situation now with my kids, I am not going to be the silly dad who just gives them whatever they want. They are going to have to embark on their own careers, whatever they may be. I will encourage and support them, but I will not give them everything. They are going to have to stand on their own two feet sooner or later, because that's what I believe in.

Whether or not they follow in my spike marks, who knows? They both love the game, but it's very much a young kid thing that they want to do what their dad does, so I will support and encourage them, but I definitely won't push or coach them. I tell the guys at Portrush what I think the boys are doing wrong, but I'm not hands on and I don't pressure them. I'm not the kind of dad who goes to the range and stands behind his boys giving advice all the time. If they're good enough, they're good enough and if they want to do it, we'll just see what happens.

However, there are certain things I want the boys to do in life in addition to playing golf, which they can do anywhere in the world and which will help them to socialise. It may sound ridiculous, but I want them to fly-fish, because they can also do that anywhere. I want them to speak a second language fluently. And finally I want them to play a musical instrument, any musical instrument, because there are times I get so envious when I go to a pub and there's a guy in there playing the piano or guitar. Those are the four things I'd like my kids to do, because they will help them get by in any situation and in any line of work they go into.

* * *

I do feel incredibly grateful and fortunate in my career, because it's one not many people in the world have the opportunity to pursue. I haven't had a sensational career by any stretch of the imagination, but I'm very thankful that the game has been as good to me as it has. It's afforded me the luxury of being able to look after other people. To me, that's more important than anything else. I can be the biggest pain in the world at times, but I'd like to think that underneath it all I'm a better person than that.

I have one major regret – smoking. I positively hate it and Conor is forever going on at me to quit. I am definitely going to have to make a big effort to stop because I know it's not good for me. I've never done drugs and the reason I've never done them is not because they haven't been offered to me, but more because I was worried that I'd like them. My nature is if it's good, have another and another – and that would not be good. I've seen guys, including multimillionaires, lose everything they possessed because of cocaine and heroin and so on. Drugs simply scare me because of my compulsive nature.

A smaller regret is that at my age I still have not discovered patience. I just can't suffer fools and occasionally I'm too quick to criticise other people's mistakes without thinking properly. I hate that sarcastic side of my nature and more than once I have had to ask myself why I've said something or not kept quiet. I don't mean any real malice by it. I never obtain the perfection in golf that I seek, yet I unreasonably expect perfection in people all around me.

* * *

All in all, my life has had its happy and sad chapters. Right now I'm content and happy with everything off the course and I'm much happier again living back at home. What's more, I'm very grateful to have the love of a good woman to keep me on the sensible path.

Professionally, I will always keep chasing the unattainable. But would I change anything? Yes, I would have loved to have won twice as much and if I was starting over again I'd work three times as hard from 100 yards and in – even though, in comparison, I reckon I've worked harder on that aspect of the game than many.

Would I change any aspect of my lifestyle, with all my toys and my extravagances and spending? Not one thing. I've worked extremely hard, rewarded myself and had a great time doing it. What's more, I appreciate just how lucky I've been to get to that position.

I'm a normal bloke really. I hope there are not many airs and graces about me now. I admit that I was, as a few journalists will attest to, rather more difficult to deal with in my earlier years. But I've mellowed some, so that I'm now just a normal guy playing golf, having a bit of fun.

My life has been and will always be an open book.

CAREER STATISTICS

European Tour Record

Year	Race to Dubai	Events Played	In Money	1	position 2	3	4 to 10	stroke average	average position	official €
1990	-	1	AM	-	-	-	-	75.08	50.00	-
1991	112	19	11	-	-	-	1	72.87	67.11	41,845
1992	41	27	19	-	1	-	5	71.89	54.30	196,412
1993	8	30	23	1	1	-	4	71.28	38.36	517,545
1994	37	21	17	-	-	-	5	71.33	42.86	208,160
1995	14	27	21	-	1	-	6	71.30	39.78	316,845
1996	8	26	18	1	-	1	3	71.45	48.27	461,713
1997	4	23	19	-	2	2	5	70.22	23.48	752,373
1998	2	18	17	2	3	1	3	69.45	22.17	1,264,014
1999	8	21	19	1	1	-	5	71.12	32.18	731,291
2000	2	22	21	2	3	2	4	70.29	18.45	2,717,965
2001	3	23	21	1	1	2	5	70.02	28.55	1,988,055
2002	22	20	19	1	-	-	3	71.01	31.20	848,023
2003	2	18	17	1	1	-	6	70.48	26.00	2,210,051
2004	8	19	17	-	-	3	4	70.56	30.21	1,563,803
2005	20	14	13	-	1	1	4	70.65	27.57	971,131
2006	43	14	12	-	-	1	2	71.43	41.36	583,348
2007	138	20	11	-	-	-	-	72.76	72.75	172,110
2008	13	29	21	2	-	1	4	70.84	48.24	1,151,038
2009	61	24	20	-	-	-	3	71.11	54.58	534,733
2010	30	28	20	-	2	-	2	70.61	49.50	892,388
2011	11	22	17	2	-	-	1	71.54	54.55	1,590,415
TOTAL	-	466	372	14	17	14	75			19,713,058

Course Records

60 (-12) Smurfit European Open	1999 (CR)
60 (-9) European Monte Carlo Open	1992 (CR)
62 (-10) BMW International Open	1992 (CR)
62 (-10) Collingtree British Masters	1995 (CR)
63 (-8) TNT Dutch Open	1998 (CR)
63 (-9) Volvo Masters Andalucia	1998 (CR)
65 (-7) GA European Open	1993 (CR)
65 (-7) US PGA Championship	2004 (CR)
67 (-5) Smurfit European Open	2002 (CR)

European Tour International Schedule Victories

Total 16

1993	Alfred Dunhill Open
1996	Linde German Masters
1998	Benson and Hedges International Open, Volvo Masters Andalucia
1999	Compass Group English Open
2000	WGC – Andersen Consulting Match Play Championship, The Compass Group English Open
2001	Smurfit European Open
2002	Compass Group English Open
2003	WGC – NEC Invitational
2004	Iberdrola Open, The 140th Open Championships

2008   BMW Asian Open, KLM Open
2011   Iberdrola Open, The 140th Open Championships

European Challenge Tour Victory
Total 1

2003   Benmore Developments Northern Ireland Masters

International Tournament Victories
Total 4

2001   Dimension Data Pro-Am (RSA), Chunichi Crowns (JPN)
2004   Mitsui Sumitomo VISA Taiheiyo Masters (JPN)
2005   Mitsui Sumitomo VISA Taiheiyo Masters (JPN)

Other Tournament Victories
Total 2

1992   Ulster Professional Championship
1994   Irish National PGA Championship

Amateur Victories
Total 2

1990   Spanish Amateur Open Championship, Irish Amateur
        Closed Championship

Teams

Ryder Cup	1997 (winners) 99, 02 (winners), 04 (winners) 06 (winners)
Alfred Dunhill Cup	1994, 95, 96, 97, 98, 99
World Cup	1994, 95, 96
Vivendi Seve Trophy	2000, 02 (winners), 11 (winners)
Royal Trophy	2007 (winners)

INDEX